COWGIRL CREAMERY COOKS

COWGIRL CREAMERY COOKS

SUE CONLEY & PEGGY SMITH
PHOTOGRAPHS BY HIRSHEIMER & HAMILTON

CHRONICLE BOOKS

SAN FRANCISCO

MIX
Paper from
responsible sources
FSC® C008047

DESIGNED BY SARA SCHNEIDER

PHOTOS ON PAGE 21 USED COURTESY OF THE STRAUS FAMILY.

THE PHOTOGRAPHER WISHES TO THANK:

*We work on many book projects, but having the opportunity to work with the ever gracious,
energetic, forward-thinking, brilliant, dynamic, fun-loving Sue Conley and Peggy Smith
was an especially gratifying collaboration. It was a pleasure and an honor to photograph
this wonderful book. We thank them for asking us to do it. We want to thank the whole
Cowgirl Creamery corral, you are a grand group! During this project, we were very lucky
to make our home base in Marshall, California, in Madeleine Fitzpatrick and Evan
Shively's charming house perched over the waters of Tomales Bay. Thank you for your
hospitality. Thank you Ann Spivack, for having such a lovely way of keeping us focused.
To the talented people at Chronicle Books: thank you for honoring the photographs.
Bill LeBlond, not by accident you publish beautiful book after beautiful book.
Sara Schneider, you design the prettiest books around.*

10 9 8 7 6 5 4 3 2 1

CHRONICLE BOOKS LLC
680 SECOND STREET
SAN FRANCISCO, CALIFORNIA 94107
WWW.CHRONICLEBOOKS.COM

This book is dedicated to Bambi McDonald, whose spirit, humor, and love of food and friends continue to inspire.

CONTENTS

Rain *rat-tat-tatted* onto the metal roof of our barn like a hail of BB pellets. It was a cold day in March 1997, just hours before the grand opening celebration at Cowgirl Creamery in Point Reyes Station. Both of us were working intently on the cleaning and final food prep for the party, when Sue said, "We're not quite ready." Peggy replied, "Nobody is going to come out to Point Reyes in this weather anyway."

But people did come. Local chefs Evan Shively and Madeleine Fitzpatrick rolled up in their pizza truck with their copper-clad pizza oven secured in the back. We could see Evan from the wide barn door, building the fire while raindrops bounced off his broad-brimmed hat.

Some of the best chefs we knew—Gail Pirie, John Clark, Catherine Brandel, Mary Jo Thoresen, and Curt Clingman—were in the back cooking, all of them pitching in to keep the food coming out for the guests.

Terry Sawyer, John Finger, and Michael Watchorn drove down from Hog Island, shuttling enormous sacks of oysters through the crowd. Within minutes, they began shucking oysters on our back counter. Kate Arding, just off a plane from London, set up an architectural display of Lancashire, Cheddar, and Stilton wheels and started cutting cheese for the people who gathered around her.

The Straus family made their way through the crowd and soon after them came Nan McEvoy, who was the president of the *San Francisco Chronicle* at that time, beside Michael Bauer, the *Chronicle*'s food editor. Then Sue's Bette's Diner business partners, Bette and Manfred, arrived, followed by some old friends who had helped us fund our cheesemaking venture and negotiate loans: Joanne Casey, Warren Wilson, John Goyak, Peter Barnes, Peggy Janosch, and Bambi McDonald.

Peggy had crafted our invitations by hand, using a charming paper cut-out of our barn, and Eleanor Bertino, who handled public relations for many famous chefs, had delved into her impressive Rolodex and mailed invitations to some of the Bay Area food mavens who had inspired us. Alice Waters was one of the first to arrive, along with a small cadre from the Chez Panisse family. Even though we had invited them, it was still a shock to see Chuck Williams and Marion Cunningham come through the door under huge black umbrellas, with big smiles for us.

The ranchers from Point Reyes and Marshall came, then the neighbors and local politicians, including Steve Kinsey and our agricultural commissioner, Stacey Carlsen; even some of the townspeople who had protested our project joined the celebration.

As the evening wore on, the room filled to capacity. We began running out of our allotment of wine and cheese, and had to pull more from our retail stock. We had emptied every bottle of wine in our store and served almost all of the cheese we had in stock before the guests began to leave. Many of the people you'll read about in the pages of this book were at that opening party.

WHY CHEESE?

In this book, we'll share how we learned to make cheese and why we were inspired to start a food business in a small agricultural town. Because both of us began our careers as cooks, we have included some of our favorite recipes and cooking techniques.

We eat a lot of cheese in the United States. Per capita, each of us eats about a pound of cheese per week, most of it grated over fast-food pizza or melted over grilled ground beef in the form of a cheeseburger. This cheese comes mostly from post–World War II factories that churn out as much as one million pounds of cheese per day with the goal of producing food as cheaply as possible.

As Americans become more aware of the unique qualities of handmade cheese, they are actively seeking small-production artisan and farmstead cheeses. "Artisan" is a term used in Europe to describe cheese made in small batches using a local source of milk. The term "farmstead" is reserved for producers who make cheese on the same property where the animals are milked. Artisan and farmstead cheesemakers are the people we'll focus on in this book. But the terms "artisan" and "farmstead" do not tell the whole story of how the dairy is managed or how the cheese is made.

HOW BIG IS YOUR VAT?

The first question we always ask a cheesemaker is "how big is your vat?" Vat size tells us the cheesemaker's scale of production; small-batch cheeses can often prove to be the most interesting. We are always on the lookout for unique regional cheeses that express the individuality of the cheesemaker and the place where they are produced. By the late 1960s, the few small-scale cheesemakers operating in America's rural communities had all but disappeared. Cheesemaking in the United States began to shift in the 1970s when the "back to the land" movement lured young people to farmland on the edge of cities. Goats were raised, cows bought for milking, and a new generation explored the art of cheesemaking. Four decades later, this small group of pioneers has inspired many cheesemakers to pursue their dream, and mentored them along the way.

Cowgirl Creamery is one of the companies that came on the scene in the 1990s, inspired by the cheesemaking pioneers of the 1970s. The first wave of artisan cheesemakers focused on honing their craft and establishing a market for their cheese. By the time we embarked on our cheese adventure, American cheeses had begun to rival the nuance and quality of the great cheeses from England and Europe, but they had unfamiliar names like Humboldt Fog, Wabash Cannonball, and Camelia. We were happy to introduce these cheeses to the marketplace at our shop in Point Reyes Station when we opened our doors in 1997. We continue to spread the word on great American cheese today.

GO WEST, YOUNG COWGIRLS!

WE HAD JUST LANDED IN PARIS after a grueling ten-hour economy-class flight from San Francisco. As we gathered our bags and hailed a taxi, we were in that strange jet-lagged state where the brain hasn't begun to process the sounds of a foreign language.

It was February 2010 and we were in France for the annual Salon de l'Agriculture, a week-long celebration that honors all aspects of French agriculture. At the Salon du Fromage, the part of the fair dedicated to cheese, we would get the chance to meet some of our French cheese idols, including shop owners Marie Cantal and Roland Barthélemy, cheesemakers from Roquefort and the Jura Mountains, and Claudine Rouzaire of Fromage de Meaux fame. Respected affineurs like Clarence Grosdidier of Jean d'Alos and Phillip Goulde from the Comté Fort St. Antoine would be there along with the best buttermakers in all of Normandy. Cheesemongers from all over the world used the opportunity to evaluate cheeses for their shop counters. For anyone interested in cheese, this was the place to be.

Just before we'd left home for Paris, an invitation arrived by email from our cheesemaker friend David Gremmels of Rogue Creamery. It said simply, "Join us at Les Fontaines Saint Honoré for a dinner with the Guilde des Fromagers." We emailed back, told David we would be happy to attend the dinner, and then didn't think about it again until the plane had landed.

Now, suitcases in hand and still dressed in the bulky knit sweaters and jeans we'd worn on the flight, we wondered if we were proper company for dinner. Before we had time to reconsider, we received an excited cell phone call from David, giving us directions to the restaurant and urging us to be on time. We dropped off our bags at the hotel, splashed our faces with cold water, and rushed to the dinner.

Les Fontaines Saint Honoré was an old-style French brasserie with gleaming dark wood surfaces and red velvet booths. We were seated with our American compatriots: Allison Hooper and Adeline Druart from Vermont Creamery, Cathy Strange, the global cheese buyer for Whole Foods, and Marc Druart, from the

Vermont Institute for Artisan Cheese. We weren't the only ones who had come from afar; importers from Japan and Singapore were at the table next to us.

The founder of the Guilde des Fromagers, Roland Barthélemy, made his rounds through the room, approaching with a big smile and a *kiss-kiss-kiss* for each of us. Barthélemy's wife, Claudine, handed us a white cardboard tube.

"What's this?" Sue shouted above the din of very loud multilanguage chatter.

Claudine's reply: "Oh, you two Cowgirls will be inducted into the Guilde des Fromagers tonight."

Both of us froze in place, staring at Mme. Barthélemy. We had thought we were just joining friends for supper. Instead, we were being welcomed into one of the most esteemed clubs of cheese professionals in the world. Up until then, so few Americans had been inducted into the Guilde that it hadn't crossed our minds we would even be considered.

"Pomp and Circumstance" began playing over the room's PA system, and the roar of the people laughing and chatting died down. A dozen tall figures dressed in brown monk-like robes and Turkish-style turbans emerged from the upstairs dining room. One by one, we honorees were invited onto the stage facing the audience. When it was our turn, David Gremmels read a list of our achievements from a scroll. There was applause, laughter, kissing, and more applause. The members of the Guilde seemed just as surprised and elated as we were to be celebrating American cheese-makers in France.

When asked to serve our cheeses, we panicked, knowing that the French would expect our service to be very proper and ceremonial. We were still trying to attune our ears to the language; it seemed to take a few seconds to decipher what was being said to us. The people that we served were among the most respected cheesemakers in the world: Sue served the table representing the Jura region, including the head of the Appellation d'Origine Contrôlée de Jura Comté, and Peggy served the head of the Appellation d'Origine Contrôlée des Pyrénées. Jet-lagged and caught off guard, we couldn't quite take in the moment. We still wore the same clothes we'd put on in California nine time zones earlier; we tried hard not to think about the fact that it was Fashion Week here in Paris. With the tall figures in robes and the crowd of smiling faces welcoming us like old friends, it felt as if we were in a dream.

The five thousand members of the Guilde des Fromagers had only recently allowed women to join, and even more recently invited Americans. That night in 2010, the Guilde added six new Americans to their roll. Four of the six were women. Two were Cowgirls.

How did we come to be on that stage? The journey began in 1971 when we were assigned to the same freshman dormitory at the University of Tennessee in Knoxville. We were both from the Washington, DC area, so felt a kinship from day one. Both of us had to find work, so we took inventory of the restaurants on the college strip and found one that looked decent with a "help wanted" sign posted in the window. We both applied to wait tables. The only hitch was that the waitresses had to work the shift in long formal gowns. Sue asked her mother to send the two prom dresses in her closet back home, and our lives in the restaurant world began.

When we weren't working, we were liberal arts students studying history and political science. Although the university was a renowned agricultural school, neither of us had any interest in the farming curriculum at that time. We were both avid music fans, and we took advantage of the fantastic folk and bluegrass concerts in the area and learned to play instruments and sing. We protested against the Vietnam War, marched for the Equal Rights Amendment, and campaigned for George McGovern for president.

After four years, we left the peaceful Smoky Mountains and headed home to find work in Washington, DC. Both of us had fallen in love with the camaraderie, theater, and energy of working on a restaurant team. Sue dreamed of opening her own place, and Peggy gravitated to professional kitchens to hone her skills at the stove. We cooked and served at various restaurants in the Washington area until we had saved enough money to buy a baby blue 1967 Chevy window van with another friend, Joanne Murray. We packed the van and headed west with about seven hundred dollars in cash in our pockets.

For six months we drove across the country, stopping for county fairs and music festivals, camping in parks and forestlands, and dropping in on unsuspecting relatives whenever we could. Along the way, we picked up a jazz singer, Rhiannon, who invited us to stay with her in San Francisco. Rhiannon lived in an old Victorian with a juggler from a small circus and an actress, high on a hill in Bernal Heights. Hello, San Francisco!

We crossed the Golden Gate Bridge on July 4, 1976, through a wispy layer of fog, and worked our way up and down the city's famous hills and into the Mission District. We landed in Dolores Park where the Alternative Bicentennial Fourth of July Celebration was in full swing. Pete Seeger sang with Malvina Reynolds on the main stage, the Mime Troupe created political theater on the lawn, and the Gay Men's Chorus led the crowd in a cheerful rendition of "God Bless America." Back home in DC, the Marine Corps Marching Band had always been the star attraction on the Fourth. A summer of the West Coast convinced us that this was where we wanted to be. Great things were happening in California restaurants, and we wanted to be part of this food revolution. We drove back to DC, worked for six months to save up some money, and then packed all our belongings and returned to the Bay Area.

This was a moment in time when Alice Waters and her innovative team at Chez Panisse were changing how people in the United States thought about restaurants. Their cooking style followed a simple philosophy popular in France:

work with the best local ingredients to create dishes that highlighted the pure, fresh flavors of the food. The ideals inherent in this style of cooking—a strong connection with the farmers and producers—echoed Berkeley's natural foods movement of the 1970s and 1980s, which aimed to push back on the industrialization of agriculture and food production. Chez Panisse was an early subscriber to the natural foods movement and one of the first restaurants in the United States to elevate simple whole grains, fresh local cheeses, and beautifully fresh vegetables to fine cuisine status. At a time when women were not welcome in professional kitchens, Chez Panisse welcomed women such as Patty Curtan, Lindsey Shere, Joyce Goldstein, and Carolyn Dille, who helped set the direction for the café. When Peggy read about Chez Panisse, she set her sights on working there.

A year after she applied, Peggy landed a job at Chez Panisse Café. In the meantime, she took classes and studied cookbooks, teaching herself classic French cooking techniques. Peggy worked in restaurant kitchens in Oregon, San Francisco, and then in the Napa Valley at the Mount View Hotel in Calistoga, where she was the breakfast and lunch cook. Another cheesemaker-to-be, Laura Chenel, worked at the Mount View at the same time as Peggy, and the two became friends.

Sue had begun studying restaurant management at City College in San Francisco and worked nights at the city's Obrero Hotel. The Obrero had a Basque restaurant famous for family-style service; guests sat at long tables and passed stainless-steel platters heaped with sliced roasted meats and mounds of mashed potatoes. The owner of the Obrero, Bambi McDonald, became our mentor.

Bambi was brilliant, funny, forceful, stubborn, and the hardest-working person either of us had ever met. Fluent in English, Spanish, Italian, French, and German, Bambi was teaching herself Swahili when we met her. As a young woman, Bambi fled the small town in New York where she'd been raised and began an open-ended adventure in Europe. She bought a one-way plane ticket to Frankfurt and over the next ten years lived in Germany, Italy, and the Netherlands. She ran a hot-dog stand in Rome and worked as a fashion designer in Munich.

While in Amsterdam, she took a job as an assistant innkeeper in a four-story *pensione,* where she learned the bed-and-breakfast trade. When her father died in 1970, he left Bambi a little bit of money. She used part of the money to move back to the States, and she chose a city with a familiar European culture, San Francisco. For the first few years, she worked as a bond broker for American Express, started a catering business, and lived with her boyfriend in a tree house on the weekends. But what Bambi really wanted to do was to run a *pensione* like the one that she'd helped manage in Amsterdam. She searched for the perfect spot and found her dream location on Stockton Street at the edge of both North Beach and Chinatown.

The Obrero Hotel was one of three Basque boardinghouses still left on a block that had once been crowded with this type of "worker's hotel." From the 1900s to the 1970s, immigrants from the Pyrénées region in France and Spain flocked to these places in San Francisco, but by the late 1970s, many of these boardinghouses had been sold to developers or fallen into disrepair. With her remaining inheritance, Bambi bought the Obrero from a Basque couple who was retiring. Bambi let the last Basque boarder keep his room and converted the other rooms for overnight visitors, mostly tourists from Europe. She kept the traditional family-style menu, and the restaurant soon had a devoted following. Bambi ran the hotel and cooked every meal. Sue waited tables and cooked side by side with Bambi, learning the ropes of running a small business.

Bambi adored food, cooking food, and talking about food. She owned more than three hundred cookbooks written in six languages. Both Sue and Peggy read Bambi's cookbooks (at least the ones in English), studying the great chefs from Auguste Escoffier and Paul Bocuse to Madeleine Kamman and Julia Child. Bambi, more than any other single person, was key to our starting Cowgirl Creamery. She inspired us, educated us, encouraged us, and supported our ideas. When Bambi died of a heart attack in 1998, she left a hole in our lives that could not be filled.

For seventeen years, Peggy worked long shifts at every station in the Chez Panisse kitchens. She cooked upstairs and downstairs and at special events including the AIDS benefit at the Greek Theatre on the UC Berkeley campus as well as dinners for President Clinton, Julia Child, and James Beard.

Peggy traveled to France to lead the team cooking at Vinexpo's California Grill for the California Vintners Association. Every other year, the Association travels to an enormous exposition where the greatest vintners in the world gather to show their wines. The Californians wanted a place where visitors could relax and focus on wines served with meals, so they added a restaurant to their pavilion and called it the California Grill.

Peggy was asked to create a menu that went especially well with California wines using ingredients local to the Bordeaux area. Peggy became friends with Chez Panisse's French chef Jean-Pierre Moullé while working with him; from Jean-Pierre she learned about cooking, ingredients, anything to do with food, and classic preparations. That carried over to Bordeaux, when Jean-Pierre introduced us to some of the most wonderful farmers and producers in the region. Through Peggy's involvement with French Cheese Week at Chez Panisse for more than a decade, she also had become friends with Pascale and Jean-Claude Cazalas from the Jean d'Alos Fromagerie in Bordeaux. With the help of Jean-Pierre, Pascale, and Jean-Claude, Peggy was able to source exceptional ingredients for the Vinexpo dinners.

Throughout the 1990s, both of us served on the cooking team of the Vinexpo's California Grill. Shopping at French farmers' markets and working with the specialty producers from the region taught us about traditional production methods, seasonality, and the importance of relationships in sourcing good ingredients. Shopping these same markets from year to year led to friendships with vendors and farmers, many of which have remained strong all these years.

Peggy was smack in the middle of America's culinary center in the 1980s, working with the region's most accomplished cooks. Napa wineries made vintages exclusively for Chez Panisse. Visiting chefs from all over the world were invited to cook in the kitchen, sharing new methods and techniques with the eager staff.

For Peggy, one of the joys of working in the Chez Panisse kitchen was being in charge of a single dish, and making that same dish individually for each guest, sometimes a hundred times in one night—egg whites whipped for a hundred cheese soufflés, a hundred lamb chops seared, a hundred rounds of Laura Chenel's goat cheese coated with bread crumbs and baked. With every order, Peggy strengthened her technique, striving to make it better each time. This method of cooking would come to serve us well while we were creating our cheese recipes.

While Peggy worked at Chez Panisse, Sue was busy building a restaurant business in Berkeley with partners Bette and Manfred Kroening. They named it Bette's Diner because Bette had the best name and was the true leader of the project.

Bette's was the first retro-diner in the Bay Area, and in keeping with the spirit of diners on the East Coast, it featured a long Formica counter with a row of stools and a dozen cozy red Naugahyde booths. In keeping with the spirit of Berkeley, a very realistic sculpture of a five-foot slice of cherry pie hung suspended from the ceiling, crafted by line cook Steve Siegelman. Breakfast was served all day to the sounds of pop hits on a chrome-trimmed vintage jukebox that played everyone from Buddy Holly to Johnny Rotten. Like any decent diner, Bette's aimed to be fast and friendly, but in keeping with the times, it used great bread, sourced fresh local produce, and made everything from scratch, including pies and scones.

The idea behind Bette's was to offer simple breakfast and lunch fare using the best ingredients available, and to make the dining room warm, welcoming, and fun. The diner was fun, it still is fun, and Bette's continues to be one of the most successful, well-run, and beloved restaurants in the Bay Area.

Bette, who had a master's degree in social work from Bryn Mawr and a job at Children's Hospital in Oakland, fell in love with cooking when she took a class taught by cookbook author Joyce Goldstein. Bette's social work skills made a big difference in our operating style when the diner opened. In Berkeley—and probably in any restaurant in the United States—the staff varies in background, nationality, religion, and culture. This makes it challenging for the person charged with helping a diverse group become a team.

Enter Rosie Cohan, an old friend of Bette's who was starting a career in management training. Rosie led us in building a harmonious team, sometimes difficult in a town that prided itself on individuality and diversity. Rosie mentored Sue, Bette, and Manfred in building a common culture at the diner. As we grew our cheese business, Rosie's teachings helped us work with staff in San Francisco, Petaluma, and Washington, DC, as well as our original Point Reyes location. At Cowgirl Creamery we've found the personality of each location varies based on the staff and regional characteristics. We've been lucky to learn much over the years from our sophisticated urban cheesemongers, our activist politicos, our Giants-loving sports aficionados (we count ourselves among them), and people who've come to work with us from Jalisco, London, Delhi, and many points in between.

After eleven years of joyful pancake flipping and egg scrambling, Sue sold her shares in the restaurant to her business partners and bought a home in bucolic Point Reyes with her life partner, Nan Haynes, a ranger stationed in the redwoods just east of Tomales Bay. A few weeks after moving into their new home, Sue heard the doorbell ring. When she opened the door, a smiling woman introduced herself. "I'm Ellen Straus and I would like you to meet the Democratic candidate for our board of supervisors." She was so cheerful that Sue invited her into the living room, where she talked for hours about many subjects, from the art show at the deYoung to the price of alfalfa. (That's Ellen on page 21.)

We wouldn't discover for some time Ellen's incredible background. Raised in Amsterdam, she and her family managed to board one of the last boats to America before Hitler's army invaded Holland. Ellen's immediate family who made it to the boat survived, but all of her other relatives who remained in Holland perished. Her family moved to Forest Hills, New York, where Ellen finished high school and was accepted into the first class at Bard College that admitted women. After graduating with a degree in chemistry, Ellen hoped to become a doctor but found that she hated the sight of blood. Ellen's aunt introduced her to an eligible young Jewish rancher, Bill Straus, who flew to New York from California for the express purpose of meeting Ellen. During their second meeting, when it was clear they shared a connection, Bill showed Ellen a photo of his ranch in Point Reyes, and they married just three months later. For decades to come, they would joke that the photo of Bill's ranch had sealed the deal.

Although her natural friendliness and warmth was what struck you first about Ellen, it didn't take long to see her strength, intellectual curiosity, and huge desire to make the world a better place. Ellen had the ability to bring people together.

During the two hours that Ellen sat in Sue's living room talking, Sue's career path took a sharp turn. Ellen talked to Sue about local dairy families going broke and how she'd become an environmentalist after reading Rachel Carson's book *Silent Spring*. Inspired by his activist mother, Ellen's eldest son, Albert, was well on his way to converting the family ranch from conventional practices to an organic dairy.

Sue knew she had to be a part of this project. When Albert (shown at far right) was ready to fill his first returnable glass bottle with certified organic milk, Sue and Ellen were standing by to help him peddle it in the Bay Area marketplace. Together, Sue and Ellen traveled the narrow, windy roads from West Marin to San Francisco day after day, talking to chefs and market managers in the city and sharing what was happening at the Straus farm. Between the milk's sweet, fresh flavors and Ellen's gregarious personality, the Straus dairy quickly developed fans who were eager to buy Straus milk.

Peggy grew to know Albert Straus as well during this time when the cooks from Chez Panisse came to the Straus dairy to learn how Albert made and packaged his organic butter. The cooks were fascinated by the wide flavor swings that could be found in Straus milk and butter. In the spring, the milk might taste more grassy and rich. A batch of milk could have a distinct mustard flavor.

Looking back on those days, it seems a bit incredible that a group of chefs would spend their days off working with an organic dairy farmer, but at the time there was a great deal of satisfaction in helping to improve the quality and availability of local food. This was our favorite part about cooking in the Bay Area in the 1980s. The people who inspired us weren't motivated by money or fame; they wanted to make something good, to create a better, healthier food system.

As Sue worked with Ellen to sell Straus milk, she was missing her days cooking at Bette's and dreamed about opening some kind of food business in Point Reyes Station. She noticed two barns for sale in Point Reyes, one a beautiful Victorian stable and the other a simple rectangular hay-storage barn, the original feed barn owned by Toby Giacomini. (The Giacominis were a prominent ranching family in the region.) Most people were attracted to the Victorian, but we agreed with our friend—and our architect—Jon Fernandez when he said he thought the simple barn was the more beautiful of the two. The simple barn had wood beams that'd been salvaged from the mill in nearby Samuel P. Taylor State Park. The old galvanized metal signs in the barn seemed to emphasize what we liked best about the town—its history, its ties to agriculture, and a straightforward approach that suited us. Jon wanted to put art studios in the barn and Sue wanted to open a food business. She could envision customers going in and out of the fifteen-foot-high wooden sliding doors on either end of the building.

Sue called Peggy and found that Peggy was ready for a new challenge, and ready to work on the business of cheese. So Peggy talked her partner Cheryl Dobbins into moving to Sonoma County to be close to the cheese. Sue agreed, on a handshake, to purchase the barn from Toby Giacomini, pending financing and permits. Jon realized he could add a second story for artists and offices, and Sue and Peggy could do food downstairs. Things were really starting to come together. Because of the work Sue had done with Ellen to sell Straus organic milk and because

of Peggy's years of working with Jean d'Alos and other internationally renowned cheesemakers and sellers, cheesemaking seemed like a logical business for us to start in that barn. While cheesemaking was new and mysterious to us, our cooking skills were something we knew we could count on. We loved the idea of creating picnic foods from local ingredients that people could carry off into the park.

Ellen's presence had a way of calming us as we struggled with the stress of starting a new business, and the stresses were many. Marin County had not seen an application for a new cheese business in fifty years, so the bureaucrats were unsure how to permit the building. When the word got out that our visitor-serving business would open in downtown Point Reyes Station, a handful of local anti-growth activists protested the permit. We spent hours preparing testimony and gathering signatures in support of our project. The public hearings were emotionally exhausting and extremely expensive, depleting our much-needed resources and energy. When we looked up, a year had gone by.

Luckily, we had secured bank financing on the reconstruction of our falling-down barn. Then, two weeks before we broke ground, the bank informed us that our loan officer had quit; we were told to submit a new application. It had taken months to put together the first application and there was no time to start from the beginning. This news sent us scrambling for private short-term loans with friends and family, which depleted all our savings and operating capital. Jon, our architect, agreed to trade his fees for an ownership share in the building, and our neighbor, environmental author Peter Barnes, also bought shares. Several friends, including Bambi, Joanne Casey, Susan Mary Seymore, Peg Janosch, and John Goyak all pitched in to help us get off the ground and give us the chance to succeed. Another year came and went but we pushed forward.

The silver lining behind these struggles was finding people who stood with us, ready to lend a hand to make Cowgirl Creamery a reality. Many community members felt that what we were doing was key to the future of farming in the area, and they worked alongside us to make it happen. One of these people, Ellie Rilla, a farm advisor with the University of California Cooperative Extension, testified on our behalf. Ellie saw that projects like ours were the catalyst needed to encourage dairy families to try to increase revenue by making cheese and other value-added products on the farm. Our agricultural commissioner, Stacy Carlsen, testified that organic agriculture was the way to go in our county and said that the Straus Family Creamery and Cowgirl Creamery could help lead in these efforts.

We had made many friends at the farmers' markets in San Francisco, Berkeley, and Marin, and now our farmer friends came from all over the region to support us. We had served (and still serve) on the board of directors for nonprofits including Marin Organic, Sonoma Marin Fair Board, and Marin Agricultural Land Trust; friends from these organizations spoke passionately about what our business would mean for the rural economy and local food production. Cowgirl Creamery was coming to represent something much bigger than making great cheese. The community was coming together around the idea of forming an appellation, of centering West Marin's regional identity around dairy farming and cheese.

Back then, Sue lived a short walk from the barn, and she was able to check in every day to see how the building was shaping up. The team peeled off the barn's metal siding and restored the wood underneath; some planks could be salvaged, others had to be replaced. The old wood in the tall sliding doors was too rotten to repair. Jon replaced the wood on each door with beautiful unplaned cedar; the wood from the old doors became high planter boxes that would hold the olive trees given to us by Nan McEvoy, whose olive ranch is a West Marin neighbor.

We worked with Jon to keep the openness and integrity of the structure—to keep it a barn, instead of breaking it up into rooms—so cheesemaking and cooking activities would take place on the perimeter with deliveries and customers sharing the wide, open middle section. The simple, straightforward design of the barn gave visitors the impression that the business inside was solid and had been there for a long time. We built on that feeling and carried it through all the new developments of business as we layered two new retail stores, a distribution company, and a second creamery on the original foundation of that old barn.

During the barn renovation, Ellen Straus would visit at least once a week, looking on approvingly as our sign was hung in place over each entrance. Ellen fit so well into the Point Reyes community that it was easy to forget she'd been raised in Amsterdam and New York. As the three of us were watching construction on the barn one day, a rider on a horse came down Fourth Street, hitched her horse to a post, and went into the local Point Reyes bank. When Ellen commented, "We live in the wild, wild West," all three of us laughed. "I guess that makes us cowgirls," Sue said, "and this must be the Cowgirl Creamery."

When we finally opened our doors three years after submitting the first permit application, we were tired, but elated. The difficulties in launching our business actually helped us in the long run, because the many county hearings forced us to reach out to our allies and to articulate the mission of our business.

THE MILKSHED CHEESE TOUR

CONTRARY TO POPULAR BELIEF, the cheese does not stand alone, and neither does the cheesemaker. The relationships we've cultivated with dairy farmers, our fellow cheesemakers, and other food artisans within our community are part of what makes our cheese (and our company) so special. The rise of artisan cheeses in the United States tells a story of how well cheesemakers have collaborated with each other and with dairy farmers. For us, and for every person who aims to make delicious cheese, it all begins with milk and the dairy farmer.

Sue was lucky enough to meet Ellen and Bill Straus, and their children—Albert, Miriam, Michael, and Vivien—just as Albert and his wife, Jeanne, were transitioning their conventional dairy to an organic dairy farm, the first certified organic dairy in the western United States. The Straus family inspired both of us to leave the restaurant world and make the leap into cheesemaking. In long conversations around the Strauses' kitchen table, we discussed milk quality, breeds of cows, organic standards, animal husbandry, and our milkshed on the Tomales Bay. (A milkshed is simply a dairy region that provides milk to a particular, mostly local community. West Marin was the original milkshed for all of San Francisco during the Gold Rush and remains an important one for San Francisco and the Bay Area today.)

OUR MILK ANIMALS

Learning about dairy farming at the Straus ranch revealed amazing new facts to us on a daily basis—like the fact that cows provide milk only after giving birth. (This is an obvious fact of life that we had never stopped to consider.)

So how do stores keep milk on the shelves all year-round? Albert and Bill Straus explained how it works at most cow dairies. The farmer divides the herd into three "strings" and rotates breeding so only one-third of the herd is pregnant at any given time. Every cow gets a few months off between births. (We breathed a sigh of relief for the working mothers at this news.)

This rest period, called "drying off," happens naturally in cows about three hundred days after they calve. Generally a cow conceives again when her calf is about a year old. This practice of rotating the birth cycles of the herd is how we can get fresh milk year-round.

The milk output from goat or sheep to cow is substantially different. A sheep produces 1gl/3.8L per day. A dairy goat may produce 1.5gl/5.8L of milk per day. A dairy cow can produce up to five times that amount. Of course, these amounts vary depending on breed, diet, and season.

UNDERSTANDING BUTTERFAT ON LABELS

Although it's a little counterintuitive, butterfat content in cheese is easily understood once you account for the water content. Most cheeses have a water content that measures between 50 and 75 percent of the cheese. Butterfat refers to the amount of fat as a percentage of solids in the cheese, once all liquid has been taken out of the equation. Why is butterfat measured this way? Cheese by its nature is constantly losing moisture. The fat content also constantly changes in small increments as cheese "dessicates," or loses moisture. For the most accurate and consistent measure of a cheese's fat, at any point in the aging process, you measure the fat content of the solids only.

On the labels of cheeses made in the United States, you see this measure noted as *IDM*, or "in dry matter." In France, this same measure appears on labels as *m.g.*, or "matière grasse."

The good news is you get to halve the number shown as IDM or m.g. fat content to know the cheese's actual fat content. When a cheese's label says "40% m.g.," that cheese has a fat content of 20 percent. We were surprised to learn that a creamy Brie, because of its high moisture content, might actually be lower in butterfat than an aged Cheddar.

HOW MILK AND CHEESE FLAVORS CHANGE WITH THE SEASONS

Some farmers choose to run a seasonal dairy, allowing their cows to give birth in the spring and dry off in the winter. Milk from a seasonal dairy will have pronounced flavor swings depending on the season. At the beginning of the lactation cycle, when the calves are first born, the milk is rich and full of life. During the last phase of the cycle, when the production is reduced, the milk is not as bright in flavor and is higher in fat and protein.

We asked Ellen Straus why the milk bought in supermarkets doesn't taste any different from month to month. She explained that most milk is blended so there aren't big flavor swings. People would be suspicious if their milk tasted floral one week, grassy the next week, and a little garlicky the week after that. Big milk producers keep their cows on feed that doesn't add strong flavors to the milk and then blend batches to make sure it always tastes the same. When we taste milk from the Straus animals, it tastes a little different every single day, and so do the cheeses made from that milk.

We make all our cheese from organic cow milk, 80 percent of it from the Straus cows. (In 2008, we began using milk from other dairies. We work with Taverna Dairy for our seasonal cheeses and Bivalve Dairy for Red Hawk.) Through years of learning about cheesemaking, we've met our share of goat and sheep ranchers and picked up some interesting animal facts along the way. Although cows seem to adjust to cycles that aren't strictly natural, goats don't shift from their natural cycle

COWGIRL
CREAMERY
turns
15

Since making their very first
batch of cheese in 1997,
Cowgirl Creamery has
depended on organic milk
from the Straus home dairy
as the main ingredient.

We raise a cold glass of milk
to our cheesemaking friends
on their anniversary.

WWW.COWGIRLCREAMERY.COM

Please rinse & return bottle
to store for deposit

quite as easily. Goat herders have learned to coax their animals into breeding in winter by placing lighted lamps in the loafing barn to mimic an early spring. This has extended the kidding season, but goats have not been so accepting of year-round breeding. And sheep—forget it. Sheep farmers have been able to extend the breeding season a little, but for the most part sheep work on nature's cycle and have their lambs in the spring. Don't try to get a goat- or sheepherder on the phone this time of year. They are just too darned busy to talk and have probably been up through the night delivering newborns in the field.

So, spring is the season when cows are released from the barns onto green pastures alive with fresh green grasses and wildflowers. It's when sheep and goats give birth and produce the richest and most complex milk of the year. For cheesemakers, the spring season marks the beginning of the dairy year. This is the best season for fresh chèvre, young goat rounds, sheep milk ricotta, and tangy fromage blanc. When spring turns to summer, the animals drink more water, the grasses are not as floral, and the milk is not as rich. This milk is perfect for long-aged cheeses that benefit from milk with lower butterfat. By summer the grasslands are drying out, so dairy animals usually get supplemental feeds such as hay, silages, and grain to keep up milk production and to keep them healthy. This brings the fats and protein levels up, and affects the flavors in the milk. This is the source of interesting, earthy notes in aged cheeses.

MAPPING THE CHEESEMAKERS

At the entrance to our warehouse in Petaluma, a large map of the United States hangs on one wall. Dozens of pastel pushpins are poked into the map, each marking a different artisan cheese company. The map is lightly speckled with pins across the Rockies and through the vast middle, with thick clusters in the East, especially in Vermont, and along the Pacific coast north of San Francisco. There is a third major grouping in Wisconsin, just south of Madison.

The map shows that small-production creameries thrive near urban centers. They sprout up close to towns with universities and farmers' markets. Cheesemakers can often find help from university agricultural advisors who are aligned with small-farm issues and can offer technical assistance to the dairies.

We've found that people in these rural communities have a reverence for farming as a way of life, and family-size dairies and cheesemakers are honored as primary contributors to the local economy and the culture. Farm issues are discussed in the local town paper, at the coffee shop, and on community-sponsored radio. Townspeople feel a sense of pride in the food that comes from their place.

When cheesemakers operate in a cluster, most naturally collaborate with each other and with other producers in the area who make on-farm goods. They might consolidate shipping or share a table at a farmers' market. This reduces costs and improves efficiencies, which in turn increases the individual producer's chances of succeeding. It also calls attention to the region as an important agricultural area, with a personality, geography, and flavor unique in the world.

Our Tomales Bay Region

The San Andreas Fault runs right through the middle of Tomales Bay, starting at the top of the Point Reyes Peninsula, through the Olema Valley, and down to San Francisco. This is earthquake country, where rich soils have been brought to the surface by tectonic movements. These pastoral grasslands have nourished beef and dairy cattle since the turn of the nineteenth century when farmers from Scotland, Switzerland, the Netherlands, Italy, and Portugal were lured west with the promise of land grants by the Mexican government.

The settlers were also assured of an immediate market for their goods. These were boom times in San Francisco. The rapidly growing population had exploded in the 1840s when gold was discovered; all those people needed to be fed. Industrious farmers on the Point Reyes Peninsula and along Tomales Bay helped to feed the growing city population. Dairy products made in Point Reyes were considered some of the best in the country and commanded top dollar in San Francisco. During the Gold Rush, Point Reyes butter sold for the alarming price of seventy cents per pound. (Considering inflation, that would translate to seventeen dollars per pound in today's market.) The dairy farmers just north of San Francisco worked hard, raised big families, and prospered.

Generations down the line, many of these same families are still working the land today, and the cheese, butter, and milk that come from our region are once again prized. But there was a time after World War II and through the 1980s when we lost many of our dairies. Many of the best historical agricultural properties near our urban populations were sold to make way for highways and housing developments. The fate of our rolling green pasturelands was further jeopardized by depressed commodity food prices. Few of America's farmers could resist selling their farms for a good price when they were going broke working the land.

Fortunately, enough people saw the Tomales Bay region as a place worth saving. In the 1970s, agriculturists and environmentalists worked together to create a national park and seashore on the Point Reyes Peninsula; a state law called the Williamson Act lowered taxes on agricultural lands; the county of Marin expanded agricultural zoning; and the Marin Agricultural Land Trust was founded by Ellen Straus and wetlands biologist Phyllis Faber to conserve the farmlands along the eastern shores of Tomales Bay. The combined efforts of forward-thinking people enabled farmers to hold on to their agricultural lands just long enough to allow the next generation to gather the skills, the financing, and the confidence to take on the challenge of producing food on that land that would command a higher price in the marketplace.

Another important group of Tomales Bay settlers, drawn by the beauty of the place, started building summer cottages on the western banks of the bay in the early 1920s. They were writers, artists, and retired professors from Berkeley and Stanford who sought refuge in the hills of Inverness. In the 1970s, young people with a pioneer spirit drifted to this far-west outpost as part of a national "back to the land" movement. They brought an idealistic community model and started a preschool, a day-care center to benefit working mothers, a health-care clinic, a community center, and a theater company. These services in downtown Point Reyes Station helped support the newest immigrants to the area, Mexican dairy workers and their families. This experienced work force was critical to the future of agriculture in the region and gave our culture a richness and vitality that energized the public schools, small businesses, and churches, all of which had been losing ground over the years.

While the large ranches were rebuilding, a handful of the new "hippie" generation started farming in the bohemian town of Bolinas. One of these young farmers, Warren Weber, helped to write the standards for organic agriculture that are still being followed today. The Tomales Bay region was an important player in the natural foods movement that the folks at Chez Panisse helped to popularize in Berkeley in the late 1970s and 1980s.

So by 1994, when we started to look at the potential for making cheese with the beautiful organic milk from the Straus Family Creamery, there was a farming infrastructure to build on and we knew that we could develop a market for our cheese based on long-time relationships with restaurant chefs in San Francisco and Berkeley, including our good friends at Chez Panisse and Bette's Diner.

Before we started making our own cheese, we'd worked with Sonoma County cheesemakers to help market their cheese as a regional collection. We reached out to Jennifer Bice of Redwood Hill Farm, Jose and Marie Matos of Matos Cheese Factory, and Cindy and Liam Callahan at Bellwether Farms. We also included the butter and milk from the Straus Family Creamery in the group. We called our marketing company Tomales Bay Foods, and when we started making our own cheese, Cowgirl Creamery became the fifth company to join.

A few years after we opened our shop and creamery in Point Reyes Station, dairyman Bob Giacomini and his family dove headfirst into the business of cheesemaking. Bob was the nephew of Toby Giacomini, who owned the Point Reyes feed barn that we bought. The Giacominis hired a cheesemaker from Iowa who was skilled in making blue, and set out to create a tart and creamy Danish-style California blue. This would be the only blue cheese made in California for many years to come, and it is indeed a great cheese. Over time, Point Reyes Original Blue has become a national favorite. Most of the milk produced on their Holstein dairy goes into the cheesemaking operation, enabling the family to increase revenues. But probably the best thing about the Giacominis' vision for producing farmstead cheese was that it brought Bob and Dean's daughters into the family business and back to the land. (You'll read more about the Giacominis on page 188.)

The Lafranchis, representing nearly a hundred years of continuous dairying in Nicasio Valley, were the next Marin family to begin making cheese. The current generation banded together to make the farm prosper. In the mid-1980s, Will and Mary Lafranchi partnered with the Marin Agricultural Land Trust to purchase what was then the Rogers Ranch. The Lafranchis bought the land while MALT bought the development rights to the ranch. Even though the family dairy had been operating since 1919, it was clear by 2000 that conventional dairy farms wouldn't stay in business much longer in West Marin. The Lafranchis began transitioning to an organic dairy in 2006, and all six of the Lafranchi siblings would play important roles in developing the family's Nicasio Valley Cheese Company, which was up and running in 2010.

The family's history in this region goes back to 1850, when Zelma Dolcini's ancestors began farming here. When Fredolino Lafranchi came to this country from Switzerland in 1910, from a region known for its aged cheeses, he recognized something of his homeland in West Marin's gently rolling hillsides. Fredolino and Zelma married in 1919, and their descendants are still making the family's renowned Taleggio-style cheese, as well as a fresh cheese, a soft ripened round, and a tomme, all reflecting the styles of cheeses made beside the mountains where Fredolino was raised.

Just northwest of the Lafranchi Ranch on the windswept shores of Tomales Bay, Marcia Barinaga and her husband, Corey Goodman, set down roots on a sprawling ranch near the town of Marshall and began raising dairy sheep for their own cheesemaking operation, Barinaga Ranch. Like the Lafranchis, Marcia was inspired by her family's agricultural heritage to make cheese: Marcia comes from a long line of Basque sheepherders and cheesemakers, and her cousins in that region of Spain today still make cheese. Marcia's grandfather, Valentin Barinagarrementeria, left the Basque village of Markina in the early 1900s and immigrated to Idaho, where he met Marcia's grandmother Eulalia Ugalde, recently emigrated from Gipuzkoa. Valentin and Eulalia married and began raising sheep for meat and wool.

Before Marcia began dreaming of making her own cheese, she and Corey were hardworking scientists, entrenched in the Bay Area's fast-paced science and technology sector. Marcia has a PhD in biology and worked as a science journalist for twenty years while Corey was a professor of neurobiology at Stanford for twenty-five years and an elected member of the National Academy of Sciences. Initially, they bought property in West Marin as a peaceful getaway, but when Marcia saw a "For Sale" sign go up on an eight-hundred-acre ranch across the road, she envisioned building a sheep dairy and farmstead cheesemaking business modeled on her cousins' operation in the Basque countryside.

Marcia and Corey represent another faction in the growing cluster of small cheesemakers on Tomales Bay. Marcia is a new farmer with a sense of purpose, financial means, and a scientific approach to the art of cheesemaking. Her exquisite cheeses are Baserri (Basque for "farmhouse"), a beautifully crafted homage to Idiazábal, and Txiki, a smaller wheel reminiscent of P'tit Basque. Marcia's cheeses are made solely from milk produced by her small flock of East Friesian dairy ewes.

Just north of Barinaga Ranch, David Jablons and Tamara Hicks, and their daughters Josy and Emmy, run Toluma Farms, a goat dairy with two hundred animals. Toluma Farms is a little different than the other ranches we've mentioned because David and Tamara have made it a priority to educate kids (not goat kids, but the other kind). During their grueling planning process, David and Tamara realized that the main mission of their working farm and creamery would be to educate children about agriculture and food production. The busloads of school children who visit Toluma every week get a chance to experience the joys and trials of working with farm animals. We look forward to meeting the next generation of cheesemakers who got their first taste of farm life right here in our milkshed.

As different as they are in background and experience, the modern-day artisan cheesemakers in our region attribute the exceptional flavors of their cheeses to the salty ocean air, temperature, humidity, and grasses that cover the hills. Fog rolls in with early morning and afternoon breezes, nurturing the sweet grasses, creating a long growing season, and keeping the humidity high—a perfect environment for the creamy texture and rich tastes of these cheeses. Today, the Point Reyes dairies have come full circle, and artisan producers are once again wowing city folk with the quality of their cheese and butter. People in the Bay Area have many artisan cheeses to choose from, with twenty-seven creameries in operation in Sonoma and Marin Counties, and more on the way.

Driftless, Wisconsin

It's called Driftless because the last glaciers that drifted down the continent glided past this part of Wisconsin, forming limestone cliffs and steep walls of earth that would come to be covered by forests while leaving a wide area of nutrient-rich soil on the valley floors. Many dairies in the region have been operating on the same land that their families settled in the mid-1800s. Amish farmers arrived here in the early 1900s, and the young organic farmers who were part of the "back to the land" movement came in the 1970s. Each influx of new farmers added to the dairy landscape.

Just as we arrived to visit our cheesemaking friends in the Driftless zone, a thunderstorm rolled in from the north. As we rounded the turn into the little town of Mineral Point and rolled up to Hook's Cheese Company on Commerce Street, the rain hit. We parked next door in front of a local potter's studio and dashed to the back of the old stone building where Tony and Julie Hook have made their cheese for decades. After two laps around the perimeter, we found an open door leading right into the room where Tony was stirring up a batch of Cheddar curds.

In this old stone creamery, there's not one modern improvement in sight. The smooth white walls are worn from years of bleach-water washing, and the grey concrete floors are hardly visible under the massive Cheddar vat. A strong and confident cheesemaker, Tony crafts big batches of familiar cheeses including Jack, Colby, Swiss, and Cheddar and has been experimenting with small batches of sheep milk cheese with Brenda Jensen from nearby Hidden Springs Creamery.

This collaboration with another dairy is what makes Hook's an important player in the Driftless cheesemaking cluster. Brenda, who has been innovative in developing unique cheeses, is an excellent marketer with a big personality and a beautiful farm that she opens up to visitors. Brenda's farm produces more milk than she can use in her cheese production. Tony is an experienced cheesemaker who has the capacity to make more cheese. When Brenda asked Tony to develop a sheep milk blue with milk from her farm, they decided each of them would sell the blue under their own brand names, and they had long conversations about what they would like the cheese to be.

In April of 2009 the first delivery of sheep milk was taken to Hook's Cheese. Tony made the cheese and then started its initial aging in one of his caves. After the first month of curing, the vats were split in half. Brenda's half was taken to Hidden Springs to cure out in Brenda's caves. The other half remained in the Hook's caves for final curing.

When they first spoke about working together on a blue cheese that Brenda had developed, both were cautious. Brenda worried that the cheese made at Tony's creamery would not be the same as hers, even though it would be made with milk from her dairy. Tony was sure that he could duplicate the cheese but was not sure it would age properly in his makeshift cave. Both worried that there would not be enough money in the project for both the cheesemaker and the farmer to profit.

Despite all their concerns, it turned out to be a match made in heaven. The Hooks sell the cheese as Little Boy Blue and Brenda sells it as Bohemian Blue. No matter what you call it, their luscious, tart, creamy blue is a winner, placing first at the 2011 American Cheese Society competition.

After meeting with Brenda, Tony, and Julie, we drove to Uplands dairy in Dodgeville, just five miles north of Mineral Point, where their award-winning Alpine-style Pleasant Ridge Reserve cheese is made on the farm by Andy Hatch and Mike and Carol Gingrich.

Uplands Cheese was started by two families, the Gingriches and Dan and Jeanne Patenaude. All of Uplands' cheese is made with the milk from their 100 percent Jersey herd. Flavors in Pleasant Ridge Reserve are sweet and nutty with notes of caramel and sea salt. When we walked through the screen door and into the bright white entryway, we found the crew seated in a semicircle on folding chairs, planning the day's production and listening to the morning news on WERN. As the door screeched shut, the guys jumped up to greet us, eager to begin the tour.

This place felt very familiar because our two companies have shared so much cheesemaking knowledge and so many ideas over the years. From the "make" room to the cool, damp aging room, where rounds of golden Pleasant Ridge Reserve rested on row after row of thick wooden boards, the sense of order and cleanliness in the facility along with the staff's camaraderie made us feel as if we were back home in California.

But Uplands does more than make award-winning cheese in their idyllic dairy. They act as a consolidator for artisan cheesemakers in their region. Local cheesemakers deliver their boxed goods to the receiving room at Uplands Cheese where Andy loads them onto pallets for delivery to distributors in New York, Chicago, and to our warehouse in Petaluma. This makes shipping more efficient and less expensive for everyone.

One of the cheesemakers who uses Uplands' consolidation services is Willi Lehner of Bleu Mont Dairy. Willi's dairy is located in Blue Mounds, just a few miles from Dodgeville, on the land where his father and grandfather farmed. Willi, who is a second-generation cheesemaker, has made farmstead Cheddars and blues for a decade and has recently added straw-bale aging caves in an effort to improve the quality of his cheese. Willi calls this "pseudo-cave aging," but in truth the environment he's created is very much like the hundred-year-old caves in France in terms of temperature and humidity and how the cheese is affected. Some of the cheeses in the cave are almost as old as Willi, made by his father while Willi (then a young kid) watched his father's techniques.

This new version of traditional aging methods—affinage—is one of a handful of similar projects taking hold in the United States. Willi's caves provide consistent humidity and ambient temperatures hovering around 55°F/13°C, the ideal temperature for cheese curing. Willi's caves are completely underground and roughly the size of a tennis court, able to hold 30,000 pounds/13,605 kilograms of cheese. This sounds like a huge inventory, but because the cheese is aged for 12 to 24 months, he will run out of space at some point if too many extra batches are added to his production. Because most of his cheese is sold directly to customers at the Dane County Farmers' Market, Willi can maximize his profit margin, enabling his business to stay small.

Most of the cheesemakers in the Driftless region sell at the Dane County Farmers' Market. This dramatic venue encircles Madison's Capitol Square and is one of the largest and most dynamic food marketplaces in the United States. Even though sales are brisk, farmers count on some revenue coming from outside the region as well.

Along with their ability to make outstanding cheese, collaboration is what's put these small-producer cheesemakers on the map. Each one of these cheesemakers is integral to making their region better known and appreciated, and together, they've created an important artisan cheese zone.

Northeast Kingdom, Vermont

Just south of the Canadian border, this dramatic mountain region is home to one of the most innovative cheese companies in America: the Cellars at Jasper Hill. Headed by the Kehler brothers, Mateo and Andy, this dairy started as a family farm with a small herd of Ayrshire cows. Initially, the brothers' goals were simple. They intended to graze cattle, raise their children, and make great cheese on farmland in Greensboro, Vermont. They acquired an old broken-down dairy located just down the road from Caspian Lake, where their family had spent many summers, and began drawing up plans for three barns, two home sites, and a milking parlor.

The desire to milk cows and make cheese was ignited by Mateo's casual encounter with the folks at Neal's Yard Dairy. As a young man, Mateo had traveled extensively through Europe and South America and happened upon the Neal's Yard Dairy Covent Garden shop in London. He asked for a part-time job and was hired first as a cheesemonger, then as a lead cheese turner in the caves over the Christmas holiday. He loved what he saw and absorbed as much knowledge and training as he could, including a cheesemaking stint at one of his favorite British producers. After several months of hard physical labor and rigorous hands-on experience, Mateo was hooked on the idea of making cheese back home in Vermont.

The Kehlers entered the Vermont cheese world as part of a third wave of food artisans. The first wave was the traditional Cheddarmakers who had thrived for generations. The second wave consisted of an energetic band of "back to the land" enthusiasts, who moved to rural Vermont in the 1980s. The most successful business coming out of this second wave was the Vermont Creamery led by Allison Hooper and Bob Reese. Allison and Bob made delicate goat cheeses, fresh cow milk cheeses, and delicious cultured butters. They opened markets in major urban areas by selling their cheese directly to restaurant chefs.

Cynthia and David Major also played an important role in this wave of cheesemakers. Their Vermont Shepherd Dairy specialized in sheep milk cheese and was one of the first sheep milk dairies in America. As demand for their rustic tommes grew, especially after the *New York Times* wrote about Vermont Shepherd Dairy tommes being the first American cheese to be sold by Neal's Yard Dairy in England, the couple expanded their capacity by using a cooperative business model that they had studied in the Basque region of France. Emulating the system used by the Basque shepherds, David and Cynthia built an aging cellar and taught neighboring farmers to milk sheep and make cheese to the Vermont Shepherd Dairy's specifications. Cheeses were made on individual farms, delivered to the cellars at the Majors' farm, and then marketed under the Vermont Shepherd Dairy label. This project helped propel many small Vermont dairy families into the world of artisan cheesemaking. (Although Cynthia left Vermont Shepherd in 2005, David still runs the dairy, now with his wife, Yesenia.)

Dairies like Vermont Creamery and Vermont Shepherd blazed a distribution trail in the early 1990s, establishing accounts along the Northeast corridor with the help of a tiny Vermont distributor, Provisions International. This was the missing link—consolidation services in a central point in the state that could deliver products from fledgling cheesemakers into populous urban centers. Later in the decade, government allies led by dairy scientists at the University of Vermont helped raise funds for a cheesemakers' training program called the Vermont Institute for Artisan Cheese. Housed at the University of Vermont in Burlington, this program helped cheesemakers across the state and the country hone their skills. By the turn of the twenty-first century, dozens of Vermont artisan cheeses were proudly featured on menus at fine restaurants from New York to Boston. Soon, the supply of handmade cheeses could not keep up with expanding demand, and big hurdles remained in getting the cheeses from the far-flung corners of Vermont to the cities along the Eastern Seaboard.

From their dairy farm at the base of the Green Mountains, the Kehlers watched financially stressed farms near Greensboro go out of agricultural use as estate buyers snapped them up. The brothers felt they had to do something about the deterioration of their local farm economy, about the shrinking population of people living off the land, and about the lack of hopeful energy in the once idyllic town of Greensboro.

Looking to Europe for ideas, Andy and Mateo sought advice from seasoned experts at Neal's Yard Dairy and from a young affineur in Lyon, France, named Hervé Mons. At Mons's cellars, the Kehler brothers observed the European practice of affinage, where an expert is charged with aging "green" cheese at a centralized facility. This expert—known as the affineur—controls the release of the cheese to market when it is at peak ripeness. It didn't take long for the Kehlers to see that this type of business would work in the Northeast Kingdom. Andy and Mateo began drawing up plans for cellars on their property for the purpose of aging their own soft-ripened Constant Bliss and Bayley Hazen Blue along with green cheeses from neighboring producers. When word of these plans leaked out into the community, representatives from Cabot Creamery came knocking on Jasper Hill's door.

Cabot Creamery Cooperative, one of the oldest and best cheese companies in Vermont, is known as a large producer of excellent block Cheddars. But after observing the growth of small-production artisan cheese companies, Cabot's cheesemakers became interested in making a traditional bandage-wrapped English-style Cheddar (also called linen-wrapped or clothbound). Although Cheddar

cheese dates back to 1170 in England, bandage-wrapping is more recent. This technique, begun in seventeenth-century England, entails wrapping the wheel of cheese in strips of linen or cheesecloth to form a barrier against bacteria. Some unwanted bacteria may cling to the outside of the wrap, but they can't penetrate and get inside to the cheese.

Knowing that the Kehlers were looking to finish cheeses, the cooperative asked Mateo and Andy to age Cabot Clothbound Cheddar in Jasper Hill's new caves. After months of meetings and discussion, the brothers agreed to partner with Cabot. It turned out that this was just the break they needed to build a grand aging complex and to keep it filled with cheese.

It took three years for the Kehlers to draw up plans, get permits, and acquire financing, but finally the massive Cellars at Jasper Hill were built on the farm. The aging of Cabot Clothbound Cheddar continues to be an important base income for the Cellars. The Kehlers are also aging cheese for a handful of local producers while continuing to expand the production and aging of their own farmstead cheeses. The long-term goal is to build a critical mass of new cheesemakers in the region, lured by the promise of training and technical assistance and, most important, affinage services for their cheese at the Cellars. The Kehlers are, in the words of Neal's Yard partner Jason Hinds, "seeking to repopulate the Northeast Kingdom with artisan cheesemakers."

ABOUT THIS CHAPTER'S RECIPES

Because we've based Cowgirl Creamery on cheese made from really good milk and because we think the flavors in good milk are underappreciated, this chapter's recipes begin with milk drinks. You'll want to make these drinks from the best local, fresh organic milk you can find.

When we were at the Salon de l'Agriculture, the same year we were inducted into the Guilde des Fromagers, we saw that the French had set up a milk bar that sold delicious milk drinks for the kids. The milk bar didn't offer lattes or cappuccinos—just fresh, wonderful milk that had been flavored with fruit purées. We loved the idea. When we opened Sidekick, our tiny lunch counter next to our cheese shop in the San Francisco Ferry Building, we decided it was the right place to offer some of those milk drinks, and we had great fun creating drinks with fresh fruit and Recchiuti chocolate.

After the milk and our constantly requested recipe for coffee, you'll find our favorite compound butter recipes. Just as with milk, you'll want to look for very fresh, organic butter whenever you can. We tend to use Straus butter, which is labeled "European-style" because it's higher in butterfat (85 to 86 percent) and lower in moisture than most standard American butters. European butters almost always list a moisture content; lower-moisture butter is better for baking and makes a firmer, creamier compound butter.

The other aspect of butter to consider when you're baking is whether or not it's cultured. Cultured butter is inoculated with buttermilk cultures, which results in a tangier flavor. Sweet butter is not cultured; look for the word "cultured" on the label. Many small regional dairies are starting to make and sell a cultured butter.

Yogurt recipes come next, and for yogurt as well, the source matters. If you were to make yogurt at home, you wouldn't add anything to it and it would likely be fairly thin. Commercial yogurts are usually thickened, typically with additives such as cornstarch or tapioca. The Straus family and other yogurtmakers who don't wish to add thickeners instead use reverse osmosis to thicken their yogurt by taking out excess liquid. Yogurt thickened this way has more of the flavors found in good fresh milk.

We like yogurt in salad dressings as well as for dips. For dressings, a thinner yogurt offers a better consistency, so don't strain it. But for dips, a thicker yogurt works best, so strain it through a paper coffee filter or cheesecloth to make it thicker and creamier before you make a dip. See how on page 58.

The last recipe in this chapter is a favorite of our customers in our Cantina in Point Reyes, a light, silky panna cotta to make when you have good fresh cream and milk and your favorite aromatic tea.

SAN FRANCISCO EGG CREAM

MAKES 1 DRINK

New York's famous hot-weather quencher, the egg cream, is made with neither eggs nor cream. The original is a simple, refreshing combination of milk, seltzer, and Fox's U-Bet chocolate syrup. On our menu at Sidekick at the Ferry Building in San Francisco, we've switched out the Fox's syrup for Recchiuti's Extra-Bitter Chocolate Sauce. (In the photo on page 51, you'll see both a San Francisco Egg Cream and the Vanilla Egg Cream variation.)

U.S.		METRIC
¾ cup	Seltzer	180 ml
1 tbsp	Simple Syrup (see page 49), cooled	1 tbsp
2 tbsp	Chocolate sauce	2 tbsp
⅓ cup	Whole milk (preferably Straus)	75 ml

Chill a pint glass. Into the chilled glass, pour the seltzer, then the simple syrup, and then the chocolate sauce. Stir vigorously. The soda will foam up to the top of the glass. Pour in the milk until the glass is full, pouring slowly so the drink doesn't overflow.

VARIATION:
For Vanilla Egg Cream, replace the chocolate sauce with 3 tbsp of vanilla syrup (see page 245).

ASK THE COWGIRLS
Shake or Stir?

PEGGY: I like to shake the egg cream in a cocktail shaker.

SUE: No, don't shake it. It'll make a mess. Stir it.

PEGGY: No, I like a nice foamy head on this, and you don't get that unless you shake it.

(Peggy pours the mixture into a makeshift shaker, shakes hard, and then laughs as drops fall onto the counter and run down her arm.)

SUE: (shaking her head) You can see why I don't like to shake it.

PEGGY: Well, maybe a better shaker is in order.

COLD-BREWED COFFEE

MAKES 11 CUPS/2.6 L

The folks at Equator Coffee, who roast coffee near us in Marin County, have made an art of getting the most flavor from coffee beans. They showed us how to brew the best-tasting coffee, using cold water. This has to brew for fourteen hours, and it's really the optimal method for getting all the flavor out of ground coffee beans without any bitterness. The best grind when brewing coffee this way is called "toddy grind." Buy fresh beans from your favorite coffee purveyor and ask for toddy grind, or use coarsely ground beans.

This recipe brews a lot of coffee. Refrigerate what you don't need for up to two days or just reduce the recipe to make the amount of coffee desired.

We pour this coffee into steamed milk for a hot beverage or make a cold coffee drink (facing page). If you want to heat the cold-brewed coffee without adding steamed milk, do it gently on your stove or in your microwave. Heat destroys the subtle flavor notes, so try not to overdo it.

U.S.		METRIC
	Two 10-in/25-cm lengths of muslin or cheesecloth	
1 lb	Coffee beans, toddy or coarsely ground	455 g
11 cups	Cold water	2.6 L

Stack the two layers of muslin so the edges align and pour the ground coffee beans into the center. Pull up the sides of the cloth and, leaving at least 4 in/10 cm to allow room for the coffee grounds to expand, tie the top tightly with butcher's twine or kitchen string. You're forming a sack with the ground coffee inside.

Fill a large lidded pot or any food-safe clean container with the cold water. Any clean glass or stainless-steel vessel will work. (Don't use a plastic food bucket that previously held aromatic foods such as pickles.) Add the cloth sack to the water. Don't stir. Push the sack under the water with your hands, and hold it there for a minute. It may rise up again but don't worry about this. Cover the container with either a lid or plastic wrap, and let it rest for 14 hours. You can do this in your refrigerator if you have room, or in any cool spot.

After 14 hours, discard the coffee sack (we empty the grounds into our compost pile), and refrigerate the brewed coffee until you are ready to serve.

COLD-BREWED COFFEE MILK

MAKES 1 DRINK

This recipe (pictured on page 51) is one of our most popular beverages at Sidekick, our lunch counter in the San Francisco Ferry Building.

U.S.		METRIC
¾ cup	Cold-Brewed Coffee (facing page)	180 ml
¾ cup	Cold milk (whole or low-fat)	180 ml
1 to 3 tsp	Simple Syrup (see page 49)	1 to 3 tsp

Combine equal parts cold-brewed coffee and cold milk, either shaking or stirring. Stir in simple syrup to taste and serve.

SPICED HONEY TEA MILK

MAKES 2 DRINKS

We like a classic blend such as English Breakfast for this spicy, yet comforting tea milk, but you can use any black tea you like. We came up with this when we bought some great spices at the Ferry Building and now make it regularly at home.

U.S.		METRIC
2½ cups	Milk (whole or low-fat)	600 ml
2	Bags of black tea	2
1 tsp	Whole cloves	1 tsp
1 tsp	Crushed cardamom and black pepper (see Chef's Note)	1 tsp
½	Vanilla bean	½
1 to 3 tsp	Honey or Simple Syrup (see facing page)	1 to 3 tsp

Pour the milk into a saucepan and heat it over medium heat. When the milk is 180°F/83°C (hot, but not boiling), take the pan off the heat and drop in the tea bags, cloves, crushed cardamom and black pepper, and the vanilla bean half. Let the mixture steep for 15 minutes. Squeeze out the tea bags and discard. Remove the vanilla bean from the milk, halve it lengthwise, and, with a small knife, scrape out all the tiny black seeds in the center. Add the seeds and the scraped bean back into the tea mixture, stir, and then strain the liquid through a fine-mesh strainer.

Stir in the honey, and serve warm.

CHEF'S NOTE:
Crush 2 cardamom pods and 3 black peppercorns together with a mortar and pestle before measuring. If you don't have a mortar and pestle, put the spices in a reasealable plastic bag, seal it, and crush them lightly with a hammer.

HUCKLEBERRY CREAM SODA

MAKES 4 DRINKS

Based on a New York egg cream (which contains neither egg nor cream), this is a light, refreshing, fizzy drink with a gorgeous color. We make this drink with huckleberries when we find them, but blueberries, strawberries, and raspberries all work beautifully. (In the photograph on page 51, you'll see a Huckleberry Cream Soda as well as a Strawberry Cream Soda variation.) This is a great use for any overripe, very juicy berry.

Everybody has a different idea of proportion for this soda. We like more seltzer and less milk, but set out the fruit purée, a pitcher of milk, and bottles of seltzer along with a cocktail shaker and a whisk (Peggy shakes and Sue stirs), and let everybody at your table fix it to suit their own tastes.

Simple Syrup

U.S.		METRIC
2 cups	Water	480 ml
1 cup	Sugar	200 g
1½ cups	Ripe, juicy berries	227 g
1 cup	Cold milk	240 ml
	Ice cubes	
3 cups	Seltzer	720 ml

To make the simple syrup: Combine the water and sugar in a small pot over medium-high heat and whisk occasionally to help dissolve the sugar. Bring it to a boil and take it off the heat to cool, just for 10 or 15 minutes. You want the simple syrup to be warm but not hot when you add the fruit to it. (You won't need all the syrup [about 1¾ cups/415ml] for this drink, but if poured into a bottle or jar and sealed, it will keep in your refrigerator for up to 6 months, ready for the next drink you'll make.)

Add the berries to the pot with the warm syrup and stir. With a slotted spoon transfer the fruit to a blender or food processor. Add 3 tbsp of the simple syrup still left in the pot to the fruit, and blend until smooth.

Pour the purée into a medium strainer or sieve set over a bowl and push the juice through with the back of a wooden spoon. You should have about ¾ cup/180 ml purée. Refrigerate the purée until you're ready to make the drinks.

For each drink—Combine 3 tbsp of the purée with ¼ cup/60 ml milk in a tall glass, either by shaking the mixture in a cocktail shaker or stirring with a spoon. Add ice cubes, pour in ¾ cup/180 ml seltzer, and shake or stir until frothy and uniform in color. Serve cold.

ICY MINT MILK COOLER

MAKES 1 DRINK

Very refreshing on a hot summer's day, this drink is best made with very cold milk and bright, fresh mint. Use a wooden muddle (like the ones bartenders use to muddle fresh mint for a Mojito) or a wooden spoon to crush the mint leaves and bring out their oil before you pour on the milk. Select a thick, heavy bar glass in which to muddle the mint.

U.S.		METRIC
	Ice cubes	
Handful	Fresh mint (leaves and stems)	Handful
½ tsp	Sugar	½ tsp
1½ cups	Very cold milk (whole or low-fat)	360 ml

Fill a heavy bar glass with ice cubes and set aside. Place the mint in another heavy bar glass and sprinkle with the sugar. With a wooden muddle, rub the sugar into the mint leaves. Add the cold milk to the glass with the muddled mint. Strain into the ice-filled glass and serve right away.

Clockwise, from top left: Huckleberry Cream Soda, San Francisco Egg Cream, Icy Mint Milk Cooler, Vanilla Egg Cream, Spiced Honey Tea Milk, Cold-Brewed Coffee Milk, Strawberry Cream Soda.

Shallot

Anchovy

Blue

Maitre d'Hotel

COMPOUND BUTTER

When you have more fresh herbs than you need, make a compound butter. If you freeze the herbed butter, it's very easy to slice off a chunk whenever you want to add flavor to fish, chicken, steaks, or vegetables. See the recipe for Blue Butter, a compound made with blue cheese, on page 203.

SHALLOT BUTTER
MAKES ABOUT 2 CUPS/455 G

U.S.		METRIC
1 lb	Unsalted butter, at room temperature	455 g
2	Shallots, minced	2
1	Garlic clove, minced	1
½ tsp	Fine sea salt	½ tsp

When the butter is soft, put it in a bowl; add the shallots, garlic, and salt; and beat with a wooden spoon until all are evenly distributed. (Taste and add more salt if needed.) Use right away or roll into a cylinder, wrap tightly in wax paper, seal in a resealable plastic bag, and refrigerate for up to 1 week or freeze for up to 3 months.

continued

ANCHOVY BUTTER
MAKES 2 CUPS/455 G

U.S.		METRIC
8	Anchovy fillets (preferably salt-packed)	8
1 lb	Unsalted butter, at room temperature	455 g
½ tsp	Fine sea salt (optional)	½ tsp

Rinse the anchovy fillets in cool water; if they have bones, remove them (see Preparing Anchovies, page 240). Grind the anchovy fillets with a mortar and pestle or in a food processor until a paste forms. Put the room-temperature butter and anchovy paste in a bowl and, with a wooden spoon, beat the paste into the butter until evenly distributed. Taste the butter, and add the salt if necessary. If you used salt-packed anchovies, it shouldn't need more salt (but if you used oil-packed anchovies, it might). Use right away or roll into a cylinder, wrap tightly in wax paper, seal in a resealable plastic bag, and refrigerate for up to 1 week or freeze for up to 3 months.

MAÎTRE D'HÔTEL BUTTER
MAKES ABOUT 2¼ CUPS/510 G

U.S.		METRIC
1 lb	Unsalted butter, at room temperature	455 g
¼ cup	Freshly squeezed lemon juice	60 ml
½ tsp	Freshly grated lemon zest	½ tsp
¼ cup	Minced fresh flat-leaf parsley	15 g
¼ cup	Finely minced shallots	55 g
¾ tsp	Fine sea salt	¾ tsp
½ tsp	Freshly ground white pepper	½ tsp

When the butter is soft, put it in a bowl and, with a wooden spoon, beat in the lemon juice, ¼ tsp at a time. When all the lemon juice has been added, beat in the lemon zest, parsley, shallots, salt, and pepper. (Taste the butter and add more salt and pepper or lemon juice if needed.) Use right away or roll into a cylinder, wrap tightly in wax paper, seal in a resealable plastic bag, and refrigerate for up to 1 week or freeze for up to 3 months.

YOGURT–PUMPKIN SEED DRESSING

MAKES ABOUT 1 CUP/240 ML

This dressing (pictured on page 57, top right) is good on a wedge of lettuce, an arugula salad, or on fresh, hot asparagus. Yogurt combined with shallot macerated in vinegar makes an easy salad dressing, at once creamy and bright. Chopped pumpkin seeds add some crunch. See Making a Vinaigrette, page 240, for why we use two kinds of vinegar.

If you'd like to liven up this dressing's color, add the tomato paste. It's not necessary but it does add a nice warm tone. Please don't use ketchup instead of tomato paste. It will make the dressing too sweet.

U.S.		METRIC
1 tbsp	Sherry vinegar	1 tbsp
1 tbsp	Balsamic vinegar	1 tbsp
1	Shallot, minced	1
⅓ cup	Pumpkin seeds	45 g
½ cup	Nonfat yogurt	120 ml
2 tbsp	Crème fraîche	2 tbsp
2 tbsp	Chopped fresh flat-leaf parsley	2 tbsp
1 tbsp	Freshly squeezed lemon juice	1 tbsp
1 tsp	Tomato paste (optional)	1 tsp

Pour both vinegars over the shallot in a small bowl. Set aside.

In a small, dry pan, toast the pumpkin seeds over medium-low heat. Toss continually, and stay close—these burn easily. As soon as you smell them, slide them out of the pan and onto a plate to cool.

Mix together the yogurt, crème fraîche, parsley, and lemon juice. Pour in the shallot and all the vinegar. Stir in the tomato paste (if using).

Chop half of the pumpkin seeds. Stir the chopped pumpkin seeds into the dressing. Reserve the remaining whole pumpkin seeds to sprinkle over the salad.

GREEN GODDESS DRESSING

MAKES ABOUT 2 CUPS/480 ML

A classic dressing, Green Goddess (pictured, facing page, left), is seeing a new popularity. Created in San Francisco in 1923 by Philip Roemer, the chef at the Palace Hotel, this dressing gets its bold, savory flavor from anchovies and its vibrancy from fresh tarragon. It's so full-flavored and such a beautiful color that it can make even a simple salad of lettuce, tomatoes, and green onions something special. This is also a great dressing for a crab salad.

U.S.		METRIC
3	Anchovy fillets (preferably salt-packed)	3
	Sea salt	
1 cup	Mayonnaise (preferably homemade)	220 g
½ cup	Nonfat yogurt	120 ml
1	Ripe avocado	1
1	Garlic clove, minced	1
3 tbsp	Minced fresh chives	3 tbsp
¼ cup	Minced fresh flat-leaf parsley	15 g
1 tbsp	Minced fresh tarragon	1 tbsp
¼ cup	Chopped green onions, white and green parts	30 g
	Freshly ground black pepper	

Rinse the anchovy fillets in cool water; if they have bones, remove them (see Preparing Anchovies, page 240). On a cutting board, use a chef's knife to mash the anchovies and 1 tsp salt into a paste. Mix together the anchovy-salt paste, mayonnaise, and yogurt and then pour into a blender, scraping the bowl. Peel the avocado, discard the peel and pit, and add the avocado to the blender. Add the garlic, chives, parsley, tarragon, and green onions and blend to combine. Season with pepper, taste, and add more salt and pepper, if needed.

Clockwise from left: Green Goddess Dressing, Yogurt-Pumpkin Seed Dressing, Yogurt-Dill Dip.

YOGURT-DILL DIP

MAKES ABOUT 1¼ CUP/300 ML DIP OR 2¼ CUPS/540 ML DRESSING

You can make yogurt richer and creamier by straining it: Just spoon it into a paper coffee filter set in a colander and then let it rest in your sink for an hour. Mix with shallot and dill and you have a nice dip for celery, carrots, jicama, and apples. If you want to skip the draining step, this mixture (pictured on page 57, bottom right) makes a light, fresh sauce for salmon or a dressing to pour over a salad of romaine, poached chicken, apples, celery, and raisins.

U.S.		METRIC
2 cups	Nonfat or low-fat yogurt	480 ml
1	Large shallot, finely minced	1
2 tbsp	Freshly squeezed lemon juice	2 tbsp
½ tsp	Freshly grated lemon zest	½ tsp
2 tbsp	Crème fraîche	2 tbsp
2 tbsp	Chopped fresh dill	2 tbsp

To strain the yogurt if making a dip: Place a paper coffee filter in a colander in your sink. Spoon in the yogurt. Let it sit at room temperature until it has the consistency of thick sour cream, 30 to 60 minutes; discard the liquid that drains from the yogurt (or you can do what our own Maureen Cunnie does: refrigerate the liquid and add it to a smoothie within 24 hours).

In a small bowl, combine the shallot and lemon juice and let it rest for 10 minutes. Then pour the shallot and lemon juice into a medium bowl with the yogurt (either strained for a dip or unstrained for a dressing). Stir in the crème fraîche and dill.

This will keep in your refrigerator for up to 3 days but may need to be stirred before using.

EARL GREY PANNA COTTA

SERVES 8 TO 10

When we make this at our Cowgirl Cantina in Point Reyes, it sells out almost immediately because it's a popular addition to a picnic lunch. This is a simple dessert, lighter and silkier than a pudding, and much easier to make. If you have good milk and good cream, this might be the best dessert to make with them. Choose a brand of Earl Grey tea that is very aromatic such as Mighty Leaf, Twinings, Bigelow, or Harney & Sons.

Sheet gelatin produces a creamier panna cotta. If you have trouble finding gelatin sheets, you can use 2 tsp powdered gelatin sprinkled over ¼ cup/60 ml cold water, but the result will be slightly stiffer and less silky, although still good.

U.S.		METRIC
2	Gelatin sheets	2
1 cup	Whole milk	240 ml
4	Earl Grey tea bags	4
2 cups	Heavy cream	480 ml
¼ cup	Sugar	50 g

Soak the gelatin sheets in a bowl of cold water for 10 minutes.

While the gelatin soaks, pour the milk into a saucepan and heat it over medium heat. When the milk is 180°F/83°C (hot, but not boiling), take the pan off the heat and drop in the tea bags. Let them steep for 15 minutes, squeeze out the tea bags, and discard them. Add the cream and sugar to the saucepan with the milk tea and heat the mixture over low heat. While it heats, gently squeeze the gelatin sheets and then add them to the warm milk-cream mixture. Stir until dissolved, and then pour the mixture through a medium-mesh strainer into a large heat-proof measuring cup with a spout.

Pour into 4-oz/120-ml ramekins (for 8 servings) or 3-oz/90-ml ramekins (for 10 servings), and chill overnight before serving.

CHEF'S NOTE:
If you heat the milk to more than 180°F/83°C, the panna cotta may form a darker layer at the very top when it sets. This doesn't affect the flavor at all, but if you'd like to avoid it, use a thermometer to check the temperature when heating the milk and cream.

THE CHEESE COURSE

A WELL-COMPOSED MEAL shows thoughtful planning: The courses should be appetizing and visually appealing, and should complement each other. The same holds true for a cheese course. Tasting is key. Before you put together a cheese course, let us share a few things that we've learned about tasting cheese.

A LESSON IN CHEESE TASTING AT JEAN D'ALOS

We gained an invaluable lesson in identifying the flavors in cheese while visiting Jean d'Alos, the renowned fromager and affineur in Bordeaux, France. Peggy had met Jean-Claude and Pascale Cazalas, owners of the shop, when she worked at Chez Panisse, so while in France, we were invited to a cheese tasting with Jean-Claude in the cellars of Jean d'Alos.

From the street, Jean d'Alos looks like a modern white storefront with an office space above, but the fromagerie is built over a sixteenth-century monastery. The medieval catacombs that lie deep underground wind all the way to the Gironde Estuary. The thick limestone walls of the catacombs are ideal for storing and aging cheese because they provide a constant, cool temperature and are porous enough to maintain natural humidity.

To further control the environments in the caves, Jean-Claude and Pascale built several small rooms on each of the three subterranean levels. The variations in humidity and temperature from one level to the next can be subtle, but the results are dramatic. The lowest floor is the coolest and most humid, perfect for mold-ripened cheeses that are fully mature. Aged cheeses are stored on the second floor, which is not quite as cool and humid. The top floor is for cheeses that require less moisture and a slightly warmer temperature.

Aged cheeses rested on row after row of thick wooden planks, stacked from floor to ceiling. The soft bloomy rinded cheeses were carefully placed on shiny stainless-steel wheeled racks. Small white paper tags dangled from the cheeses and the shelves; handwritten notes on these tags told the history of each cheese including make date; receiving date; turning schedule; washing, brushing, or other treatment; and any maintenance the cheese had received. We saw hundreds of shelves with two dozen cheeses on each shelf and thirty rolling steel racks with ten shelves on each stack. We were counting in our heads, thinking that there were at least two thousand cheeses and each of them had to be turned, brushed, and pampered until the experts deemed them ripe and ready for the shop.

Seeing the cheeses in these caves was like seeing a Titian painting in a church instead of a museum. The mottled rinds of the cheeses showed every color imaginable. The damp odors in the caves ranged from bacon to porcini mushrooms, and we could hear the sounds of dripping whey and the hum of refrigeration. Many of the cheeses were as heavy as stones, and the old wooden boards creaked under their weight. This was where cheese was meant to quietly age away from heat and light.

Jean-Claude led us under thick limestone archways into a dimly lit stone cellar, where a huge wheel of cheese, 3 feet/1 metre across, rested on a massive marble slab. He announced that we would be tasting the king of cheese, a three-year-old Comté made in the Jura Mountains. The cheese had a beautiful rind, fawn-colored with the feel of a sturdy felt hat. Behind the cheese, a dozen glasses were filled with a dry sherry the color of golden raisins.

Jean-Claude explained that Comté is made by many satellite groups of small cooperatives called *fruitières,* and that it has been produced in the same manner for hundreds of years. By the rules of the AOC—the appellation d'origine contrôlée, the French certification granted to a product such as cheese, butter, or wine that follows the traditions and geographic rules as set by the French government—the milk for the Comté cheese must come from a Montbéliarde cow. This breed is low to the ground and quite hardy, making it ideal for steep mountain regions. Farmers milk their cows twice a day and then take their milk to the fruitière, which is generally within 8 miles/13 kilometres of the farmer's dairy.

When the milk reaches the fruitière, cheesemakers must make the wheels of cheese in the large traditional copper vats, and all of them must follow the same guidelines for cheesemaking procedures, the cultures, rennet, and cheese size. Usually eight to twenty dairy farmers work with each centralized cheesemaker. There are as many as fifty cheesemakers, each working with a cluster of farmers within the Jura region, and throughout the region there are 175 fruitières.

Even though the process is the same, each of those cheesemakers produces a cheese with a flavor profile that is slightly different from the next cheese. This makes comparative Comté tastings important to affineurs and brokers like Jean-Claude and Pascale. Flavors in the cheese change with the seasons because the milk flavors depend on what the cows are eating. The profile flavor traits, however, remain true to the fruitière.

The last element of production is the affinage, or the aging of the cheese. This takes space—Comté cheeses are heavy and large and require at least 10 months of aging—so cheesemakers work with affineurs who age the cheeses off-site. Affinage determines the quality of the cheese and is just as important as good milk and the cheesemaker's skills.

Most of the Comté produced in this region is aged in old military forts on the peaks of the Jura Mountains. These stone forts are massive, and naturally cool and humid, so when they were abandoned in the mid-1900s, local cheesemakers recognized a better and higher use for them. The cheese we were about to taste was aged in one of these old forts, Fort St. Antoine. Just this fort alone houses more than eighty thousand wheels of cheese, and each wheel is turned and washed weekly. Prior to the 1980s, a team of workers was required to wash, brush, and turn each wheel of cheese by hand. These days, robots do the heavy lifting. The robots grab a cheese wheel off the two-story-high wooden racks and wash, brush, and turn each cheese before replacing it on the shelf.

We thought about this particular cheese's life as Jean-Claude took out his cheese iron, a long, thin metal wand. He used the handled end to lightly tap on the cheese, beginning at the outer rim and working in a concentric circle until he reached the center. He was listening for cracks or fissures that would indicate imperfections in the paste. The tone remained consistent, so Jean-Claude could assume the cheese had no apparent flaws. He plunged the iron into the middle of the cheese's side, pushing until its tip reached the center of the wheel. He twisted the iron and slowly withdrew it from the cheese. He held up the iron to show us that it contained a perfect cross section of the Comté, from the rim to the center.

He inspected the cheese sample closely, then drew the iron under his nose, inhaling the cheese's fragrance. He broke a snippet of cheese off the very end of the iron and gave that little piece a sniff, explaining that much of the flavor of the cheese comes from the aroma, which intensifies as the cheese reaches room temperature. To help this along, he lightly rolled the small bit of cheese between his thumb and index finger, noting its texture, and whether it felt smooth or grainy. When the cheese had been warmed by his fingers, he popped the small bit into his mouth and spread the cheese over his tongue as well as the roof of his mouth. He breathed in and out, waited a minute, then described the many flavors he tasted in this one tiny bite of cheese.

Jean-Claude passed out samples from the core for all of us to taste in the same manner. Even though we'd tasted cheeses for years, this method widened our experience in a way that was startling. We learned to detect waves of flavors and to pay attention to the subtle aromas and textures. Then we tasted again, this time with a sip of sherry. The sherry brought out the fruit flavors in the cheese, and the cheese highlighted the savory notes in the sherry. The aromas in the dim, damp cave, the way the enormous wheel of cheese filled the space, the flavors that rose and receded as we tasted—this experience still informs how we taste cheese.

Peggy demonstrates the method of cheese tasting that we learned from Jean-Claude Cazalas in Bordeaux.

roasted
pineapple

nuts

Chocolate

oyster
shells

lemon verbena

bacon

brown butter

honeycomb

chamomile

meyer lemon

flowers

wet stones

scalded milk

green garlic

caramelized onions

PLANNING A CHEESE COURSE

When you plan a cheese course, think about how cheese is tasted at Jean d'Alos. The first step is finding a cheesemonger willing to serve you bites of a few different cheeses. No, you won't have the dimly lit limestone caves or the glass of sherry, but you can close your eyes and try to tune out everything around you while you taste.

What's the first flavor that comes into your mind when you taste a cheese? You can use that initial flavor to set up what we call the Zuni Café method of cheese pairing: Find a single flavor or nuance in the cheese and look for an accompaniment that brings out that flavor. (More on this in "Consider the Zuni Method," page 79.)

Think of your cheese course as an opportunity to understand cheese. To our way of thinking, cheese has as much complexity in flavor, texture, and intrigue as menu items that contain five, ten, or twenty ingredients. A cheese course can be illuminating when you start with excellent cheese and a point of view. What do we mean by point of view? Structure your cheese course to answer a question and to deepen your understanding of cheese. Maybe you'd like to know how three different Cheddars—each from a different region—taste when compared to each other. Or maybe you'd like to know how the same cheese tastes at different steps in the aging process. Or maybe you'd like to know how three different cheeses taste with a wine that you particularly like. When you choose cheeses that illuminate some aspect of cheese for you, a cheese course can live in your memory the way the tasting at Jean d'Alos has stayed with us.

TIPS FOR PLANNING A CHEESE COURSE

START WITH A POINT OF VIEW
See "Twelve Points of View for a Cheese Course" (facing page) for ideas on how to structure a cheese plate.

SHOP AT A STORE WITH A CHEESEMONGER
The first step in creating a balanced cheese board is to shop at a place that has an attendant at the cheese counter. This person, the cheesemonger, is responsible for procuring and caring for the cheese at the shop and should offer tastes, impart knowledge, and guide you to appropriate cheeses that fit the season, your budget, and your point of view.

WORK WITHIN A BUDGET
Buy only enough for the cheese board (and a week's supply of leftovers). The cheesemonger can suggest cheeses within any budget. When we select cheeses for the mail-order catalog, we sometimes splurge on one exotic cheese and make the other two less expensive, more familiar cheeses. You can do the same when creating a cheese course at home for guests.

STORE CHEESE PROPERLY

If your cheese comes wrapped in plastic, unwrap it and throw the plastic away. Cheese should be wrapped in wax paper or butcher paper and then stored in the refrigerator, away from the fan. Don't hold on to it for longer than a week. Parmesan Broth (page 236) is a great way to use the last bits of cheese on hand. (See The End Bits, starting on page 207, for more ideas.)

SERVE CHEESE AT ROOM TEMPERATURE

Subtle flavor notes will be lost if the cheese is served cold. The day you plan to serve, take the cheese out of the refrigerator in the morning, unwrap it, and put it under a cheese dome (or a bowl turned upside down). This allows some air exchange while protecting the cheese from natural enemies such as insects, sunlight, or sneaky pre-party snackers. It usually takes three hours to bring cheese up to room temperature, but if you can leave it out of refrigeration for six to eight hours it's even better. (But if the weather is hot, plan on a shorter warming period.)

ARRANGE THE CHEESE COURSE TO SUIT THE CROWD

A well-balanced cheese board is a versatile and visually enticing offering before dinner, with cocktails, or at the end of the meal. Cheese can be passed, arrayed on a plate, or displayed as part of a buffet.

Twelve Points of View for a Cheese Course

Here are a few points of view that you can delve into with your tastings. These are not all the points of view you can pursue, but just a few that we've tried with success. If you are searching for specific types of cheeses—say a cheese made from the raw milk of a Jersey cow in Italy—you can try the search engine in our library of cheese. Go to www.cowgirlcreamery.com and click on "Library of Cheese." You can select the farm or cheesemaker if you know it, the milk type, country, and milk treatment.

1. CONSIDER THE MILK

At least a few times a week we host tastings that start with three simple, fresh cheeses: one made from cow milk, one from goat milk, and one from sheep milk. This is an excellent way to get a sense of how the flavors differ from milk to milk, highlighting the milk's sharp or high tones.

You can follow this idea with aged cheeses, too. Selecting three aged cheeses of a similar style, each made with a different milk, highlights the deep tones of the milk. Younger cheese brings the bright milk flavors forward, while aged cheeses express these differences in more muted ways.

Or, try serving three milk cheeses that are made in a similar style with milk from the same type of animal, but different breeds, such as a mountain tomme from the Montbéliarde cows of France, one from the milk of a Vermont Tarentaise herd, and one from the Valdostana cows of Val d'Aosta in Italy. You'll notice the subtle differences in milk produced by the different breeds in different parts of the world.

To taste cheeses within our own appellation, we'll often set out Cowgirl Creamery Fromage Blanc (cow), Redwood Hill Farm Fresh Chèvre (goat), and Bellwether Farms Ricotta (sheep). These cheeses aren't made with identical processes—we add crème fraîche and salt to our fromage blanc while the ricotta has a cooked curd—but they're close enough to give you a sense of each milk's flavor.

WEST COAST FRESH CHEESES MADE WITH DIFFERENT MILKS
Cowgirl Creamery Fromage Blanc (cow)
Redwood Hill Farm Fresh Chèvre (goat)
Bellwether Farms Ricotta (sheep)

AGED CHEESES; SAME TYPE OF MILK; THREE DIFFERENT COUNTRIES
Comté, milk from Montbéliarde cows of France
Tarentaise, milk from Tarentaise cows of Vermont
Fontina Val d'Aosta, milk from Valdostana cows of the Italian Alps

2. A VERTICAL FLIGHT OF CHEESE

A vertical tasting—a common practice in the wine world—can work for a cheese course, too. Set up a vertical course with at least three examples of the same cheese at different stages in aging. For example, try a single producer's bandage-wrapped Cheddar at 12 months, 18 months, and 24 months of age.

Because the milk, the cheesemaking process, and the aging environment remain constant, vertical tastings reveal the subtle differences in the cheese as it ages. Taste the cheese from youngest to oldest, and note changes in color as well as flavor and aroma. Because it can be a challenge to find very young cheeses from Europe, try three American producers for these flights.

THREE VERTICAL FLIGHTS
Bandage-Wrapped Cheddar: 12, 18, and 24 months
Wagon Wheel: 2, 3, and 4 months
California Crottin: 2, 4, and 8 weeks

3. A HORIZONTAL FLIGHT OF CHEESE

Try a horizontal cheese tasting—cheeses from different producers but made in the same style and aged the same length of time. The differences stand out when you taste the cheeses side by side. The characteristics of the milk, the humidity and temperature in aging, the skill of the cheesemaker and the affineur, and, finally, the care of the cheesemonger where the cheese is purchased—all these elements affect the flavor. Taste to see which similarities and differences you detect when you serve cheeses in horizontal flights; see which region's version you like best. Keep in mind that flavors change; serve cheeses from the same dairies one year later and the flavors can be very different.

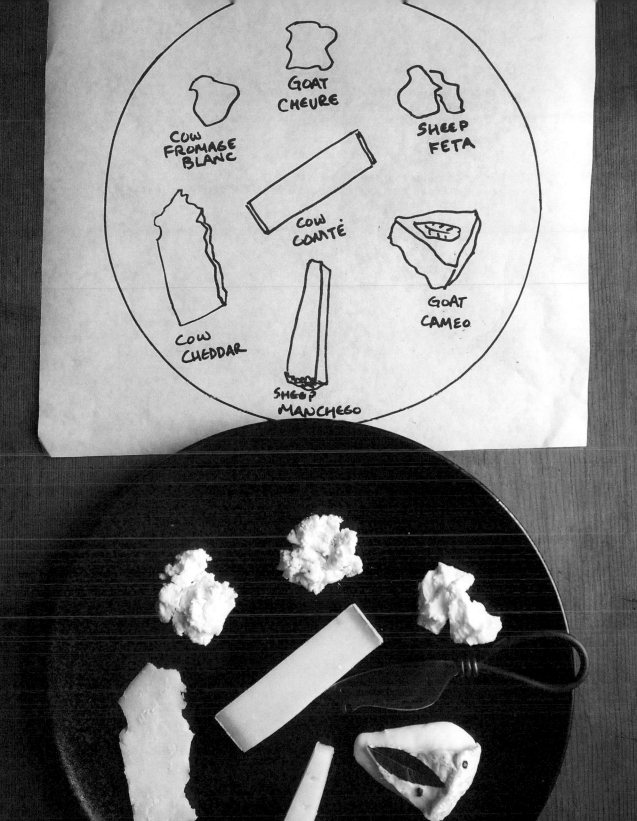

GOAT
CHEVRE

COW
FROMAGE
BLANC

SHEEP
FETA

COW
COMTÉ

COW
CHEDDAR

GOAT
CAMEO

SHEEP
MANCHEGO

HORIZONTAL FLIGHT, VERY ACCESSIBLE: AGED CHÈVRE
Taupinière, Laura Chenel's Chèvre, California
Hoja Santa, Mozzarella Company, Texas
Wabash Cannonball, Capriole, Indiana
Humboldt Fog, Cypress Grove Chevre, California

**HORIZONTAL FLIGHT, SOMEWHAT ACCESSIBLE:
BASQUE-STYLE SHEEP MILK CHEESES FROM DIFFERENT BREEDS OF SHEEP, EACH
CHEESE AGED ABOUT 6 MONTHS**
Ossau, French Basque, Manech and Basco-Béarnaise ewes
Idiazábal, Spanish Basque (hardwood-smoked), Latxa ewes
Baserri, Barinaga Ranch, California, East Friesian ewes crossbred
　　with Katahdin
Vermont Shepherd, Vermont Shepherd Dairy, Vermont, East Friesian
　　ewes crossbred with Tunis and Dorset

**HORIZONTAL FLIGHT, CHALLENGING TO ACCESS: COMTÉ FROM DIFFERENT FORTS,
OR FROM THE SAME FORT BUT DIFFERENT PRODUCERS**
(For this flight, you'll need to work with a cheesemonger who knows
quite a bit about the various fruitières who make Comté cheese.)

4. CONSIDER THE SEASON

This might be the easiest cheese course to purchase. Get some help from your cheesemonger by asking which seasonal cheeses are ripe and ready, and go from there. A
horizontal flight of seasonal cheeses is simple to set up: Just choose three or five
examples of the same cheeses made by different producers in the same season.

HORIZONTAL SEASONAL FLIGHT, SPRING
St Pat, Cowgirl Creamery, California
Freya's Wheel, Briar Rose Creamery, Oregon
Hillis Peak, Pholia Farm, Oregon

5. CONSIDER TEXTURE

Creamy, crumbly, smooth, dense, grainy, and curdy are a few words that describe
cheese textures. It's eye-opening to arrange cheeses with a variety of textures on
the cheese board. The differences in age, milk, production, and rind treatment all
play an important role in the final texture of a cheese. Try designing a cheese
course composed of three fresh cheeses with three different textures—cottage
cheese, fresh sheep ricotta, and fresh chèvre—and taste the cheeses first on their
own and then drizzle one with good olive oil, one with sweet pepper relish, and
one with honey. This is a delicious way to explore the textures and finishes left
behind by various milks.

　　You can also explore texture by serving a fresh young cheese beside an aged
cheese from the same milk. For example, a creamy fresh chèvre can be served with a
young aged goat cheese like Humboldt Fog. Fresh and young cheeses offer a good
starting point in understanding texture.

AGED CHEESE: FIVE DIFFERENT TEXTURES
Vacherin, Switzerland (very rich, sticky interior)
Classico (goat Gouda), Tumalo Farms, Oregon (dense, smooth)
Mt Tam, Cowgirl Creamery, California (smooth, creamy)
Lancashire, England (buttery crumble)
Parmesan, Italy (dry and flaky)

6. CONSIDER THE REGION

Regional flavors are well known in the wine world, where regional characteristics are clearly defined. Planning a cheese course around specialties of a region conveys a sense of the place's culture and personality. Creating a tasting with cheeses from the regions of coastal California, southern Oregon, or western Washington, for instance, will highlight the flavors that the air, soil, water, flora, and grasses of a place all impart to the cheese.

Look for types of milk used for making the cheeses in the region, the typical styles and sizes that are most prevalent, and whether the area's population supports small producers. Creating a regional cheese course connects you with the area's agricultural history. Wherever we find ourselves in the world, we always shop at farmers' markets first to develop an understanding of local cheeses. Here are four regions to explore; don't limit yourself to these!

NORTHERN CALIFORNIA
Cameo, Redwood Hill Farm
San Andreas, Bellwether Farms
Nicasio Square, Nicasio Valley Cheese Company

VERMONT
Oma, Von Trapp Farmstead
Dorset, Consider Bardwell Farm
Cremont, Vermont Creamery

SOUTHWEST FRANCE
Tome de Bordeaux, Jean d'Alos
Gabietou, Gabriel Bachelet
Tomme du Couserans, Jean Faup

NORTHERN ITALY
Taleggio, Bergamo
Ubriaco, Veneto
Pecorino Ginepro, Emilia-Romagna

7. CONSIDER THE RIND

The rind speaks volumes about the paste inside. If the rind is in good shape, it has been doing its job of protecting the cheese as it ages. The rind tells where the cheese is in its life, how it's been cared for, whether it has been washed or brushed evenly.

Some rinds are made of mold; some are natural, waxed, or foiled. The smell, texture, and evenness of the rind offers the first clue as to what flavors await beneath the skin.

Try building a cheese board with five cheeses all with similar rinds but made from different milks. Another approach would be to show three cheeses of the same age and type, but finished with different rinds. You could also taste three cheeses made by different producers in a similar style from the same milk and with the same rind treatment.

Cheeses with Similar Rinds Made from Different Milks

BLOOMY RIND
Mt Tam (cow), Cowgirl Creamery, California
Camellia (goat), Redwood Hill Farm, California
Nancy's Shepherd (sheep), Old Chatham Sheepherding Co., New York
Valsetz (goat), Rivers Edge Chèvre, Oregon
Camembert Vermont, Blythdale Farm, Vermont

WASHED RIND
Tomme d'Aquitaine (goat), Jean d'Alos, France
Taleggio (cow), Arrigoni, Italy
Red Hawk (cow), Cowgirl Creamery, California

BLUE CHEESES OF THE SAME MILK AND AGE WITH DIFFERENT RINDS
Colston Bassett, Blue Stilton, England
Point Reyes Original Blue, Point Reyes Farmstead Cheese Co., California
Rogue River Blue, Rogue Creamery, Oregon

DIFFERENT PRODUCERS, SAME MILK AND RIND TYPE
Bandage-Wrapped Cheddar, Fiscalini, California
Clothbound Cheddar, Cabot Creamery Cooperative, Vermont
Flagship Reserve Truckle, Beecher's, Washington

ASK THE COWGIRLS:
Do you eat the rind?

PEGGY: Most French people never eat rind. It's merely a skin, there to protect the cheese as it ages.

SUE: I often eat the rind. Many of the rinds are so beautiful—like one rind we make with stinging nettle. Eating that adds to the pleasure, for me.

Is there any rind you wouldn't eat?

SUE: There are a few rinds I wouldn't eat. None will make you ill, but some cheese rinds—those that show the bore holes of cheese mites, for example—might not be very enticing.

8. CONSIDER YOUR BEVERAGE

We hesitate to respond when people ask which cheeses to serve with specific wines. Because both wine and cheese are so variable, our recommendations change from season to season and with different vintages.

Start by selecting a wine that you really like. Consider its flavors: Is it light or heavy? Is it fruit forward or does it have strong mineral flavors? Does it have a low or high alcohol content? After answering these questions, choose cheeses that can either bring forward the wine's nuances or complement them. Don't be afraid to try three or five or seven different cheeses and discover for yourself which cheese tastes best with your wine. Some of the cheeses may not work with your wine, but that's not the end of the world. It's fun to taste and see what works.

You can do this with beer, tea, or cocktails as well. After years of tasting, we've developed a few general preferences.

DRY SAUVIGNON BLANC AND VIOGNIER
Perhaps the best choice for the widest range of cheeses

WINES HIGH IN TANNINS SUCH AS CABERNET SAUVIGNON
Harder to pair with cheese because tannins can create a bitter aftertaste

DRY FRUITY RED WINES SUCH AS PINOT NOIR OR SYRAH
Work well with most cheeses

WINES WITH OAK FLAVORS SUCH AS CHARDONNAY
Strong oak flavors can overpower the nuances in cheese

ALE OR HEARTY BEER
Aged Cheddars are a natural choice

SHERRIES
Alpine-style cheeses such as Comté or Emmenthaler

PORTS AND MADEIRA
Blues, soft-ripened cheeses

HARD PEAR OR APPLE CIDER
Aged sheep or cow cheeses

FLORAL TEA (CHAMOMILE OR JASMINE)
Young aged goat cheese

GENMAI CHA (WITH OATY AND YEASTY FLAVORS)
Many longer-aged cow or sheep milk cheeses, especially ones with sweeter notes

CHAMPAGNE
We like Champagne with almost all cheeses

What's your favorite beverage to serve with cheese?

PEGGY: It depends on the cheese. At a food event in Atlanta, we did a tasting with six beers and Mt Tam as well as a few other cheeses. I was worried that Mt Tam would be too rich and milky with beer, but these pairings were surprisingly successful. The cheese forms a platform that lets you taste more clearly the beers' individual flavors. We tasted a stout, an India pale ale, a porter, a lager, and a wheat beer, and the only one that didn't work really well was the wheat beer. I was surprised by how well all of them worked with a ripe triple-crème. So beer can be a good choice.

As for wines, if I had to generalize, I like Pinot Noir and Syrah because they're softer and more fruit forward. Fruit notes balance well with cheese if it's a softer type of fruit such as raisin flavors or cherry flavors.

SUE: Champagne complements beautifully the tangy notes in fresh goat cheeses and soft-ripened cow and sheep milk cheese. Because Champagne tends not to fight the bolder cheeses, it's a wine that works universally.

I also love a big, fruity Zinfandel with the sharpness of an aged Cheddar or Gouda.

9. CONSIDER YOUR AUDIENCE

Give the cheesemonger a profile of your guest list and consider a cheese course that is relevant to that group of people. Are they bold cheese explorers, sophisticated travelers, professional chefs, relatives from China? For example, if serving guests visiting from France, we'd serve cheeses made in the United States. We'd make up a diverse plate using all the different milks and choose cheeses that we knew something about so we could talk about the farms or the producer. If serving people not accustomed to cheese, choose really accessible cheeses. The following cheeses have easy crowd-pleasing flavors:

> Mt Tam, Cowgirl Creamery, California
> Mimolette Extra Vieille, Normandy
> Humboldt Fog, Cypress Grove Chevre, California
> L'Amuse Gouda, Northern Holland
> Barely Buzzed, Beehive Cheese, Utah

Purchase the right amount of cheese for the number of people expected. When composing a plated cheese course to be served at the end of the meal, cut a piece that has at least 1 ounce/30 grams per person. If serving cheese at a cocktail party, plan on 2 ounces/55 grams of each cheese per person. You might have leftovers; see the recommendations in The End Bits, starting on page 207.

ASK THE COWGIRLS

How many cheeses are best on a cheese plate?

SUE: We would say one, three, or five. Tasting one cheese is a fine way to focus on all the flavors in a single cheese. Two cheeses leave something to be desired; it's more interesting to compare and contrast three cheeses. You could serve cheeses with three different textures, or the same cheese at three different ages. Plus there's a design consideration behind using an odd number of cheeses instead of an even number.

PEGGY: I agree that three cheeses look better on a plate than two. There's a lot to be said for trios in cheese. You find three types of milk—cow, goat, and sheep. There are three primary divisions in texture—hard, medium, and soft. So having three cheeses gives you a better contrast, and as Sue said, there is a design element to having three instead of two.

Tasting more than five cheeses is difficult. Just as in wine tasting, after a certain point your ability to detect subtle flavors is not as acute. There are exceptions to this rule. For a very focused tasting in which you're seeking specific flavors in the cheeses, you'll want to serve at least six to eight cheeses. The Cheat Sheet tasting, next, shows how to do this.

10. CONSIDER A FOCUSED TASTING WITH A "CHEAT SHEET" PLATE
When we teach a tasting class, we'll often set out five to eight classic cheeses along with a "cheat sheet" plate. See the photograph on pages 66–67 for some of the aroma and flavor aids that we use for this type of focused tasting. Include foods with flavors or aromas that are found in cheese, including bittersweet chocolate, button mushrooms, nuts, caramelized onions, roasted pineapple, and truffle salt. (Be sure to taste the truffle salt last, at the very end of a tasting, because its flavor lingers.)

Because aroma contributes so much to a cheese's flavor, we like to bring "aroma aids," such as slate, hay, or straw. If you bring some spring hay that still shows some green as well as completely golden late-harvest straw, you'll be surprised by how different the two smell.

If you can't get your hands on hay, fresh clippings of lawn grass can provide an interesting smell. These are just to give you the idea of fragrances that are so common we don't even think about them; yet when you focus on their fragrance you can find it more easily in what you're tasting.

A little water can amplify the fragrance of these aroma aids. Pour water over the slate and breathe in the fragrance. Stuff some straw into a wide-mouth glass jar and pour in a couple of fingers of cool water, and then pass the jar so everyone can get a whiff. When you encounter this same sensation in a cheese, you'll have a moment of recognition that's very satisfying.

Here's an eight-cheese focused tasting that we've used several times. Have guests taste cheese in this order, from top to bottom, and identify which flavors from the "cheat sheet" can be found in each cheese.

> Fromage Blanc, Cowgirl Creamery, California
> Mt Tam, Cowgirl Creamery, California
> Comté, Jura Mountains, France
> Baserri, Barinaga Ranch, California
> Terra, Redwood Hill Farm, California
> Red Hawk, Cowgirl Creamery, California
> L'Amuse Gouda, Northern Holland
> Queso de la Serena, Extremadura, Spain

11. CONSIDER CHEESE AS A MEAL IN ITSELF

Think of the cheese course as a stand-alone meal. Serve any perfectly ripe cheese with some sliced and lightly toasted delicious bread, a variety of olives dressed in fresh herbs and olive oil (Seasoned Olives, page 87), a handful of lightly dressed salad greens, and a glass of a bright Sauvignon Blanc.

12. CONSIDER THE ZUNI METHOD

Cheese didn't even get a mention on most San Francisco restaurant menus when Judy Rodgers, chef at Zuni Café, added a cheese course to her menu in the early 1990s. Even more unusual was the way Judy structured the cheese course, and she still does it this way. Each week, she selects three cheeses and pairs each with one perfect accompaniment. Sometimes it's a young goat cheese paired with arugula dressed in peppery olive oil. Another course might be a cross-sectioned slice of a piquant blue cheese with ginger-poached pear slices and pomegranate. Choosing an accompaniment that coaxes out nuances is a beautiful way to understand and appreciate the flavor profile of just that one cheese.

mostarda

dates

mustard

olives

nuts

membrillo

raisins

crackers

apricot

honey

chutney

fig cake

preserves

ASK THE COWGIRLS

Can you give me a few tips on finding the perfect accompaniment to a cheese?

PEGGY: Taste the cheese when you buy it. Close your eyes when you first taste and see which flavor comes to mind first. Either accentuate a flavor that you find in the cheese or choose a food that works to contrast that flavor. For example, sheep milk cheese usually has sweet, nutty flavors. Candied nuts can work really well. Or you can pair in the opposite direction. You could pair a goat milk cheese that's a little salty with something sweet, maybe poached fruit, which can draw out the sweetness that's hard to find when you taste the cheese on its own. Then, when you taste the cheese you might find a whole new flavor—salt, sweet, and a combination of the two.

SUE: Try not to overthink this one. It's hard to go wrong with accompaniments like roasted nuts and dried fruits. Remember that a strong, salty blue cheese or a sharp Cheddar begs for sweet and tart fruits like apples and pears. Rich cheeses like Camembert and Brie are nice with spicy greens, a drizzle of good olive oil, and salt. Look at our accompaniments (photograph on pages 82–83), prepare a few of them, and see which one works.

ROASTED ALMONDS WITH SMOKY PAPRIKA

MAKES 2 CUPS/250 G

Almonds seasoned with just three ingredients—olive oil, sea salt, and the smoky paprika known as pimentón de la Vera—take just minutes to make but taste so much better than standard almonds.

When roasting nuts, stay nearby. They seem to heat very slowly and then, when they reach the right temperature, can turn too dark very quickly. You want to take the nuts out of the oven and get them off the baking sheet as soon as they've roasted through, but before they burn.

Try using different types of paprika, sweet or hot; they'll turn out well as long as your spices are fresh and aromatic.

U.S.		METRIC
2 tbsp	Extra-virgin olive oil	2 tbsp
2 cups	Raw almonds	250 g
¾ tsp	Paprika (preferably pimentón de la Vera)	¾ tsp
¼ tsp	Sea salt	¼ tsp

Preheat the oven to 350°F/180°C/gas 4. Line a baking sheet with parchment paper.

In a medium bowl, drizzle the olive oil over the almonds and toss. The almonds should have a light gloss of oil but not be drenched. Sprinkle on the paprika and salt, and toss again. Spread the almonds in a single layer on the prepared baking sheet.

Bake for 5 to 8 minutes, but don't rely on the clock. The nuts are done when you can smell the almonds and when a nut is warm all the way through when you taste it. Don't let the nuts burn.

As soon as you take the pan from the oven, pour all the nuts onto a cool baking sheet or a heat-proof platter, spreading them so they cool more quickly.

These nuts will keep for 1 month if sealed in an airtight container in a cool, dark spot.

ROASTED FIGS

MAKES 4 FIGS, ENOUGH FOR 4 PEOPLE

Roasting intensifies the flavor of a fig. It works well for Adriatic and Black Mission figs, but Turkey figs really benefit from a short time in a hot oven.

A sprinkle of balsamic vinegar brings out the sweetness in the figs. You can roast as many or few figs as you like—just plan on one to two figs per person.

As part of a cheese course, we like to serve this alongside Onion-Garlic Confit (page 88) and pickled red onions (see page 155) to balance sweet with savory and sharp flavors.

U.S.		METRIC
4	Fresh figs, halved	4
4 tsp	Balsamic vinegar	4 tsp
	Sea salt	
	Freshly ground black pepper	

Preheat the oven to 450°F/230°C/gas 8. Arrange the fig halves in a baking dish, cut-side up. Drizzle each fig half with about ½ tsp balsamic vinegar. Bake just until the figs are hot through, about 7 minutes. Don't let them get too brown or dried.

When you take them out of the oven, sprinkle with a little sea salt and black pepper before serving.

SEASONED OLIVES

SERVES 8

Warming and seasoning olives is a simple way to enhance their flavor. This method uses an easy trick: Rinsing your olives first, and then rolling them in a clean towel, helps them absorb more flavor when you pour on warm oil and seasonings. Don't let the olive oil get too hot. The oil should never reach a point where it's too warm for you to dip in a finger and taste.

When we think of olives and olive oil, Nan McEvoy comes to mind. Nan makes some of the best estate extra-virgin olive oil in the world, just north of the Golden Gate Bridge. If you're lucky enough to find McEvoy Ranch Nuovo Olio, it's the essence of the fall harvest from her ranch. The way Nan started her olive grove says a lot about her. Inspired by a holiday in Tuscany, she imagined that the hills of her Marin County ranch could support the same trees. After intense research, when she had a sense of which trees would do best on the sunny steep hillsides of Petaluma, Nan shipped six Tuscan bare-root olive varietals directly from Italy. These days, many of the new olive tree plantings in Northern California come from McEvoy Ranch. By propagating her trees and selling to other ranchers, Nan has single-handedly seeded a new specialty crop on Marin's Coast. She inspires us with her sensibilities, aesthetics, tenacity, and grit.

U.S.		METRIC
2 cups	Any variety of olives (preferably with pits)	360 g
¼ cup	Extra-virgin olive oil	60 ml
2	Thin slices fresh lemon (with peel), cut into small triangles	2
Pinch	Red pepper flakes	Pinch
1	Whole rosemary sprig, separated into small sprigs	1
Pinch	Fresh thyme	Pinch
Pinch	Sea salt	Pinch

Rinse the olives in cool water and set in a colander in the sink to drain. Roll the olives on a clean towel to dry them.

In a medium saucepan, heat the olive oil over medium-low heat with the lemon triangles, red pepper flakes, and rosemary sprig. Add the thyme and salt and decrease heat to low.

Add the olives to the warm oil. Heat just until the olives are warmed through.

Transfer the olives to a bowl with a slotted spoon to serve. Reserve the oil, and if there are any olives left over, store them in the oil in your refrigerator.

ONION-GARLIC CONFIT

MAKES ABOUT 2 CUPS/450 G

An onion confit is lovely with just about any kind of cheese. So savory and full-flavored, confit is like bacon without the guilt. We use this as the base for our vegetarian version of French onion soup, called panade (see page 162).

Patty Curtan, a wonderful cook who is also the designer responsible for the fruit and vegetable prints associated with Chez Panisse, once said to Peggy, "If something gives you more flavor by cutting it a specific way, then that's what you should do." We think of those words whenever a particular method of cutting or slicing yields greater flavor in the end. Here, thinly slicing the whole, peeled garlic cloves adds real depth to this confit's flavor. Slice the garlic crosswise into very thin oval slices, not from tip to tip.

U.S.		METRIC
1 tbsp	Extra-virgin olive oil	1 tbsp
1 tbsp	Unsalted butter	1 tbsp
2	Medium yellow onions, peeled and sliced into half-moons	2
4	Medium garlic cloves, thinly sliced crosswise	4
½ tsp	Chopped fresh thyme	½ tsp
Pinch	Sea salt	Pinch
2 tbsp	Dry sherry or brandy	2 tbsp
1 tsp	Sherry vinegar	1 tsp

In a large sauté pan, heat the olive oil and butter over medium heat. When the butter is bubbling, add the onions to the pan. Cook, stirring often, until the onions begin to appear translucent, about 8 minutes. Add the garlic, thyme, and salt and cook, stirring constantly, until the onions and garlic begin to show some color, about 5 minutes. Don't let the garlic become too dark or it will give your confit a scorched flavor. (If you need to walk away from the pan for a moment, decrease the heat.)

When the onions are soft and show a good amount of brown, deglaze the pan with the sherry, scraping the browned bits from the pan's bottom with a wooden spoon. Cook until the liquid is almost all evaporated from the pan, and then stir in the sherry vinegar and take the pan off the heat.

This confit will keep for up to 3 days covered in the fridge, but the flavor becomes a little less bright every day. Some people store confit in the freezer; we don't because we don't like how freezing affects the onions' texture.

ROASTED PLUM-PORT CHUTNEY

MAKES ABOUT 1 CUP/225 G

We like to serve this alongside Red Hawk with slices of levain, but it's also a good addition to a grilled cheese sandwich (see page 225) or a flatbread sandwich (see page 157).

U.S.		METRIC
4	Large red or purple plums, pitted and cut into wedges	4
1	Shallot, finely chopped	1
¼ cup	Packed brown sugar (either dark or light)	30 g
2 tbsp	Port	2 tbsp
2	Whole star anise	2
1 tsp	Cardamom seeds (preferably fresh from the pod)	1 tsp
1 tsp	Vegetable or canola oil	1 tsp
	Sliced levain bread, for accompaniment	
	Cheese wedges, for accompaniment	

Preheat the oven to 425°F/220°C/gas 7.

Gently toss together the plum wedges, shallot, brown sugar, port, star anise, cardamom, and vegetable oil. Spread evenly in a 9 in/23-cm baking dish. Roast, turning the mixture every 10 minutes or so with a spatula, until the plums are very soft, 25 to 30 minutes.

Remove the dish from the oven. Remove and discard the star anise. Using a potato masher, coarsely mash the plums.

Serve warm with bread and cheese, or refrigerate for up to 2 weeks.

FRESH CHEESES

RANDOLPH HODGSON AND THE FOLKS AT NEAL'S YARD DAIRY in England inspired us with their mission. Randolph started Neal's Yard to provide a showcase for the traditional English cheeses that were on the verge of disappearing. Under Randolph's direction, the company was dedicated not just to preserving a traditional food, but also to increasing the public's awareness and appreciation for it.

Neal's Yard Dairy buys cheese from dozens of cheesemakers in the United Kingdom and Ireland and sells it at their two shops in London as well as exporting it to shops and restaurants all over the world. There might be an ocean between us, but philosophically we stood beside Randolph and his team's work.

In 1995, we had the opportunity to see Neal's Yard in action. Randolph introduced us to his staff and showed us the various components of his business: the cheesemaking facility, the retail shop, the aging rooms, and the wholesale department. It was eye-opening to see the many facets of the business, all centered around the goal of creating a market for traditional English cheeses and supporting a livelihood for the people who made them.

A light went on for us during that trip. We looked at each other and said, "We could do that, too—we can find cheesemakers in California and create a venue where their products can be sold!"

That visit to Neal's Yard was important for another reason: It marked the first time we actually made cheese. When we asked Randolph if we could see cheesemaking in action, he grinned and said, "Sure. Be in Kent at 6:00 A.M. tomorrow." Before dawn we braved the streets of London with Kate Arding from Neal's Yard as our guide. When we reached the stone cottage where Neal's Yard's fresh cheeses are made, we suited up in white coats, hair bonnets, and white Wellies. That ritual is ingrained in us now, but at the time we found the getup very amusing.

We arrived at the creamery a few hours after the milk had been inoculated with lactic acid cultures, a cheesemaking step that we'll explain shortly. When we stepped up to the vat, the liquid had transformed into a solid yogurt-like curd with a thin layer of liquid whey on top. We immediately began ladling the curd into plastic forms pocked with little holes. We spent the next few hours refilling the molds as the whey slowly drained out, and we did plenty of cleaning in between. The whole process took about three hours. That was it! It was illuminating to realize that cheese could be made so easily, and by a single person. Not only was the operation simple enough for a solo cheesemaker, but because she'd started so early, the one cheesemaker on duty was finished by noon, at which point she talked us into joining her at the local pub, The Fox and the Hound, for a pint.

Leaving London aboard the brand-new Chunnel train leading to Vinexpo in Bordeaux, we began to write our business plan. That trip would go on to benefit us in another way: Kate Arding, intrigued by our mission, would leave the London cheese world a few years later to join us at Cowgirl Creamery.

A LOOK AT CHEESEMAKING THROUGH THE
EVOLUTION OF COWGIRL CHEESES

In this chapter and the next, we'll describe what we learned as we developed each of our cheeses. As you read, you'll get a sense of what is required to craft each type of cheese, and the many choices the cheesemaker has to make along the way.

You can make this section of the book interactive (in a very low-tech and delicious way) by having these cheeses next to you and tasting as you read how they're made. There's nothing like smelling and tasting to better retain new cheese-making knowledge. We'll explain how we make fromage blanc, fresh cheese, quark, and cottage cheese. Then we'll explain our soft aged Mt Tam and Red Hawk, before moving on to Wagon Wheel, our longest-aged cheese. We learned to make these cheeses one at a time, over more than a decade, but if you look at the evolution, you can see how our cheesemaking skills developed along with our cheeses.

The most basic piece of cheesemaking information is this: Most cheeses are made with just four ingredients—milk, salt, bacterial cultures, and a coagulant. With adjustments in temperature, humidity, cooking time, cultures, salting, aging time, and rind development or by adding ingredients such as herbs and spices, cheesemakers can create endless varieties of cheese.

Making Our First Cheese: Fromage Blanc

Years before we began making cheese, we joined the American Cheese Society, an organization dedicated to helping America's artisan cheesemakers connect with each other and learn to make better cheese. Every year, the group met on a college campus in the summer, took over the dorms, and held cheese lectures and work-shops. The people attending these sessions were academics, farmers, retailers, and cheesemakers. Each of these groups brought their own perspective on the struggle to introduce unknown domestic cheeses into a market dominated by classic cheeses from Europe. At one of these meetings we met two of America's pioneer cheese-makers, Barbara Backus and Paula Lambert, who each graciously invited us to come visit their cheesemaking operations.

Barbara lives on a tiny farm in the Napa Valley, where she and her husband, Rex, keep their goats and make cheese. We understood why Barbara and Rex call their farm Goat's Leap the second we drove onto the property: We could see goats dancing and gamboling down the hill, following Barbara on their morning walk across the farm's dry grass slopes, through the blackberry bramble, and into the milking parlor.

It's easy to see these goats are well treated. Barbara even names her exquisite, delicate cheeses after her goats. As the animals lined up for their morning milking, we were shaking our heads in wonder at how small Barbara's operation was, and how simple. This petite woman with her flock of twenty Alpine and Nubian goats makes some of the best cheeses that we had ever tasted, in a smaller space than the average-size living room.

Barbara's generosity in sharing her knowledge kick-started us on our own cheesemaking path. When Barbara bought a larger cheesemaking vat, she offered to sell us her old one. Mounted to a painted steel frame, the vat had a government-mandated recording thermometer attached to one side and a miniature hot-water heater clamped to the other. Rex, who's an engineer, had rigged up this contraption for Barbara when she began making cheese, and she had used it for eighteen years.

We jumped at the chance to buy her tiny vat, sure that it would bring good juju (an important element in cheesemaking) into our creamery. The best part of the deal was that the equipment came with lessons. Barbara invited Sue to spend a week at Goat's Leap working in the creamery, stirring the curds, and washing the tools and cheese forms. In the hours between coagulation and scooping, Barbara shared many ideas on process and procedure, the most memorable being her parting advice: "Just do it. Your place will help make the cheese."

According to Barbara, the only way to make cheese was to learn how the milk and curds behaved in your own environment. Point Reyes is cool and damp all year around; the Napa Valley is hot and dry in the summer and cold and dry in the winter. Our cheeses would behave differently than Barbara's not only because the milk was different, but also because of the wild bacteria in the air. The humidity and the temperature in Point Reyes would play an important role in the flavors our cheeses would develop.

A LITTLE CHEESEMAKING SCIENCE

So it was in Barbara Backus's tiny vat that we made our first batches of fromage blanc in Point Reyes. This is a good point to explain some of the science behind our cheesemaking. Once you know just a few terms, you'll be well on your way to comprehending the processes that take place during cheesemaking: pasteurization, lactic acid, mesophilic starter cultures, thermophilic starter cultures, coagulant, cooked and uncooked curd, double-crème (and triple-crème). We'll explain what each of these terms means in context over the next few chapters.

Every cheese we make begins with pasteurized milk. To pasteurize means to heat a food to a specific temperature as a way of killing harmful bacteria. There are several ways to pasteurize; we use a slow-vat method.

Next, let's look at lactic acid. Just as there are beneficial microorganisms at work when you make bread, yogurt, beer, or wine, so are there helpful microbes at work in cheesemaking. *Lactococcus lactis,* commonly known as lactic acid bacteria, ferments lactose (the sugars found in milk) into lactic acid. For centuries, this commonly found bacteria has assisted humans in making Cheddar, Colby,

Camembert, Roquefort, Brie, cottage cheese, buttermilk, sour cream, kefir, cucumber pickles, and sauerkraut. In fact, this little microorganism is so helpful that it's been nominated to be the state microbe of Wisconsin! It has our vote.

Although lactic acid bacteria are naturally found in milk, cheesemakers inoculate liquid milk with cultures such as *Lactococcus lactis* and other microorganisms to speed up the process and introduce flavors. "Inoculate" simply means to add to starter cultures, usually by pouring them into the liquid milk. These cultures help the cheesemaker control how the cheese will form and ripen. Enzymes in *Lactococcus lactis* digest lactose, leaving behind lactic acid as a by-product. The lactic acid is part of the reason milk separates into curds and whey (the coagulant plays a larger role) and it lowers the acid balance. The flavors and aromas in cheese are the result of biochemical changes *Lactococcus lactis* and other culture species make to liquid milk.

Mesophilic and thermophilic starter cultures are the most common lactic acid bacteria used by cheesemakers, and many cheeses use both families of these cultures. The primary distinction between the two is where they work best: Mesophilic cultures work in moderate heat and are slow acting, while thermophilic cultures are active at higher temperatures and continue to develop in the aging room. Although cheesemaking traditions have been handed down over centuries, part of the art of cheesemaking is experimenting and finding the flavors and textures that emerge depending on which cultures you use and the natural factors at work in your cheesemaking environment. Natural factors can include humidity, pollen in the air, the grasses eaten by the animals that produce your milk—all of these affect the cheese.

Barbara taught us that, in her cheeses, lactic acid works as the primary coagulant and also brings tart and buttery flavors to the milk. Other acids such as lemon juice or vinegar can be used to coagulate the milk, but will not intensify milk's natural flavors.

We noticed that Barbara added a drop of rennet to the milk along with the culture. Rennet is a fast-acting enzyme that encourages the proteins in milk to link together and bond, causing liquid milk to form into a solid or gel-like mass.

In many fresh cheeses, such as fromage blanc, this coagulation is caused by the lactic acid cultures, but the addition of rennet helps the protein molecules bind evenly throughout the liquid, which means the curd sets more uniformly. Too much rennet will cause the curd to lose its tender texture and smooth consistency. And if the curd sets too quickly, the delicious flavors will not have time to develop.

You can make your own fresh cheese using the same steps we used to make our first cheese, and then we'll explain cooked curd and uncooked curd.

Sue demonstrates how to make fromage blanc.

MAKING YOUR OWN FROMAGE BLANC AT HOME

MAKES APPROXIMATELY 1½ LB/680 G

The milk for cheesemaking needs to be fresh—no older than 48 hours. Ask at your grocery store when milk is delivered and try to buy it the same day. You will need two pots for this recipe: an 8-qt/7.5-L pot for the milk and a 2-qt/2-L pot for the buttermilk. Including crème fraîche adds a richer flavor and smoother consistency.

U.S.		METRIC
4 qt	Fresh whole milk (pasteurized or raw)	3.8 L
4 cups	Pasteurized buttermilk	960 ml
1 drop	Rennet	1 drop
2 tsp	Kosher salt	2 tsp
½ cup	Crème fraîche (optional)	120 ml

First add 1 tbsp bleach to a large pot or sink full of cool water and use it to sanitize all equipment, including bowls and spoons. Even in a home kitchen, you need to take this step because bacteria present on the equipment can prevent your cheese from setting.

In an 8-qt/7.5-L pot, heat the fresh whole milk to 90°F/32°C. (If using raw milk, pasteurize it first by heating the milk to 145°F/63°C and adjusting your stove heat as needed to keep the milk at that temperature for 30 minutes, stirring constantly.)

In the 2-qt/2-L stainless-steel pot, heat the buttermilk to 90°F/32°C. Gently stir the buttermilk into the whole milk. While still stirring, add the rennet. Stir gently for 2 minutes, making sure that the rennet and buttermilk are evenly distributed. Take the pot off the heat, cover it, and wrap it in a large towel to keep the milk at a stable temperature. Let the wrapped pot rest in a warm place for 10 to 12 hours. A turned off oven is a good place to set the curd.

continued

By morning, the milk should have set and will have the texture of a very firm yogurt. Line a colander with cheesecloth or muslin and rest it over a large pot. Using a mug or plastic tub, scoop the curd into the colander and allow to drain for at least 1 hour or up to 4 hours, until the curds have drained to a soft, smooth consistency. When they are ready, turn the curds into a stainless-steel mixing bowl and add the salt. Stir in crème fraîche (if using). Store in an airtight, nonreactive container made of plastic, glass, or stainless steel. The cheese will keep in your refrigerator for up to 10 days but is best eaten within a few days.

You've just made a simple lactic-acid coagulated cheese; the lactic acid in this cheese is in the buttermilk.

Our Second Cheese: Quark

In the early months, while Ellen Straus was helping us scoop the fromage blanc curd, she was also insisting that we add a cheese called quark to our repertoire. Ellen's husband, Bill, remembered quark very fondly from his childhood in northern Germany. Quark is more tart than fromage blanc and has a smoother, silkier texture, almost like a thick yogurt. Ellen was confident we could make a fine California version. The procedure for making fromage blanc and quark is the same, but the bacterial cultures that we added were different and we made the quark with skim milk instead of whole milk.

To achieve this flavor profile, fast-acting thermophilic cultures found in yogurt were mixed with the slow-acting mesophilic cultures found in buttermilk. Because thermophilic cultures work quickly at higher temperatures, they often create stringent flavors with a really clean finish—it has a lot in common with yogurt's flavors, which makes sense, as the same bacteria are added to both. After draining the curd in cheesecloth sacks, we added just a hint of salt, further distinguishing the soft, spreadable quark from its creamy cousin fromage blanc, which has more salt.

Our Third Cheese: Cottage Cheese

The third and most complicated fresh cheese that we learned to make was cottage cheese. This is where you'll learn the difference between cooked and uncooked curd.

The difference between handmade small-vat cottage cheese and machine-made cottage cheese is striking. Handmade cottage cheese isn't uniform; the curds are small, uneven, and very tender and flavorful. But finding handmade cottage cheese can be difficult.

All cottage cheese curd is made with skim milk set with mesophilic cultures. After the curds are drained, they are tossed in a "dressing" that can be formulated with a butterfat content that can range from 0 to 30 percent. (The fat content of the cottage cheese dressing is something the cheesemakers get to decide.) We make our dressing from a clabber, which is a cooked and cultured cream. That's why our cottage cheese is labeled "clabbered cottage cheese."

Because it looks like simple fresh cheese, you might think that cottage cheese would be as simple to make as fromage blanc, but this isn't true: Cottage cheese is downright finicky. We could make our lives a whole lot easier by adding rennet to the milk along with the cultures, which is what industrial manufacturers do, but we don't add rennet because it toughens the curd. Large-scale manufacturers make cottage cheese by the ton in huge closed vats with the push of a button, using milk that is pooled from many dairies. Cheese made that way doesn't have any hope of achieving the same nuances of flavor that we get from our meticulous small-batch process using milk from one exceptional local organic dairy.

To keep our cottage cheese very tender, we set the milk with lactic acid cultures only, pouring the culture into the warm milk at 4:00 P.M., allowing it to set overnight, and then cutting the custardy curd at 6:00 A.M. After cutting the curd into cubes, which releases the liquid whey, we stir it carefully for an hour or more while bringing the temperature up slowly. The whey becomes warm enough to cook the curd. As the curd slowly heats, more whey is released. When the mixture reaches the required temperature, half the whey is drained off and the exposed curd gets a shower of shockingly cold water. This stops the cooking while rinsing the curd of lactic acid, transforming the tart flavors into sweet and clean-tasting curd.

There you have it: Cooked curd just means heating the curds and whey up to a temperature where the curd gently cooks in the liquid whey.

Getting cottage cheese to set right takes practice and patience. Factors as simple as too much pollen in the environment or unusually cool air temperatures can slow down the setting of the curd, forcing the cheesemaker to adjust cooking and stirring times. When a cheesemaker-in-training is skilled enough to make cottage cheese without supervision, we know they've reached a certain level of expertise. Learning to carefully stir and cook the curd gives a cheesemaker their first glimpse into making aged cheeses. Most aged cheeses, including Cheddar, Parmesan, and Gouda, begin with cooked curd.

Our First Big Failure: Rindless Cheese

In our early days, when much of our cheesemaking was trial and error, not all of our experiments were successful. Our most costly experiment was inspired by a request for organic fresh mozzarella from the chefs at Chez Panisse. The chefs were eager to buy more than 100 pounds/45 kilograms of mozzarella per week, which seemed to us an opportunity too good to ignore. Paula Lambert of the Mozzarella Company in Dallas, Texas, generously opened her doors to show us the ropes.

When we flew to Texas, we traded San Francisco's summer fog for a monster heat wave in Dallas. The weather couldn't have been more different from cool, misty Point Reyes, but it had a lot in common with summer in Naples, Italy, where stretched-curd cheeses were invented. Stretched curd—or *pasta filata*, as the Italians call it—means a cheese that is stretched and kneaded like bread dough at a precise point during cheesemaking. This action, together with the pH balance of the curd, gives mozzarella its elastic texture.

Paula's enthusiasm is as boundless as all of Texas, so when we pulled up to her tidy green building, and she ran out to greet us in bright red lipstick and white Wellie boots, we were excited at the thought of learning her technique.

Our excitement turned to amazement. Making mozzarella might appear simple on a cooking show, but making a sufficient amount by hand is labor-intensive and difficult to get right. The process starts with culturing the milk, setting the curd, and then cutting it into big cubes. Cheesemakers stir the curd slowly at first and then immerse the silky mass in steaming hot water and stretch it as quickly as they can. Paula had developed a method that allowed for a sequence of thirty batches of cheese to be stretched every ten minutes.

Once the curd in the first vat reached proper acidity (5.2 pH), it was tipped into a copper kettle and worked with a long wooden paddle until the mass became smooth. Warm water was added, a little at a time, until the curd reached a taffy-like elasticity. The strand was cut into chunks, which were plopped one by one into small stainless-steel bowls where fresh hot water was poured over the curd. Behind each bowl was a woman stretching the curd into perfect egg-shaped balls and dropping them one by one into a cool bath. Eight women worked at once, each stretching continuously. All thirty small batches (1,200 balls) were completed and ready for packaging before lunch. Watching this operation, both of us had sinking hearts; Paula's cheesemaking was very different from the pace and energy of our cheesemaking back home. Paula's batches were much bigger than ours, there were many more employees in one room than in our Point Reyes barn, and speed was of the essence.

We thanked Paula for her generosity and headed home. On the plane, Sue compared the notes from our Dallas experience with our cheesemaking bible at that time, *Cheese and Fermented Milk Foods*. In the chapter on soft Italian cheeses, our cheesemaking guru, Frank Kosikowski, had this to say about mozzarella, "Mixing and molding are extremely important parts of mozzarella cheesemaking but perhaps no more important than other steps. Improperly conducted on unsuitable curd, the results will be loss of one's sanity." In Dallas, we learned that the last stretch is only part of the process. When you see chefs making mozzarella on television, they are only doing this final stretching step. The difficulty comes in making the curd, which most chefs who "make" mozzarella actually buy.

After two years of making mozzarella, Sue finally threw in the towel. (And Sue never throws in the towel.) The curd was inconsistent. It was either too tough or too soft. Hundreds of sad mozzarella balls, too poor to be sent to clients, stood as witness to the hours wasted and the money that went into troughs when our cheese failures were used as animal feed. Once in a while, Sue will casually mention that she might give mozzarella-making another try. "Maybe the climate is too cool here or our milk is too rich? We could adjust for those things." Peggy's response is always calm and consistent. She'll turn to Sue, raise her eyebrows, and ask, "Are you insane?"

COTTAGE CHEESE PANCAKES WITH CRÈME FRAÎCHE AND STRAWBERRIES

SERVES 4; MAKES 16 TO 20 (3-IN/7.5-CM) PANCAKES

Sue tossed many a pancake during her eleven happy years as a breakfast cook at Bette's Oceanview Diner. This is one of her favorite pancake recipes. You'd expect the cheese to make the pancakes heavy, but the opposite is true. During cooking, the cheese and egg whites work together to make these light. You can use cottage cheese or ricotta.

Sue still sees the folks at Bette's. When we began making cheese in Point Reyes, Bette's switched over to Cowgirl Creamery cheese and became one of our best customers.

U.S.		METRIC
1 pt	Strawberries, halved	300 g
½ cup	Sugar	100 g
6	Eggs, separated	6
½ cup	Whole milk	120 ml
1½ cups	Cottage cheese or ricotta cheese	340 g
½ cup	All-purpose flour	60 g
½ tsp	Kosher salt	½ tsp
1 tbsp	Sugar	1 tbsp
	Vegetable oil, for the griddle	
4 tbsp	Melted unsalted butter	55 g
	Crème fraîche, for accompaniment	

In a medium pan, toss the berries and sugar over medium heat until the sugar dissolves. Set aside.

In a large bowl, beat the egg yolks until thick. Add the milk and beat for another 30 seconds. Gently fold in the cottage cheese.

In a separate bowl, sift together the flour, salt, and sugar and pour into the cheese mixture, stirring lightly.

With an electric mixer or whisk, beat the egg whites on medium-high speed until they are stiff but not dry. Gently fold the whites into the batter, just until combined.

Heat a lightly oiled griddle or skillet over medium-high heat. Ladle ¼ cup/60 ml of the batter onto the hot griddle for each pancake, leaving space between pancakes. Cook until bubbles appear on the surface of the pancakes, then flip.

When done, spoon on berries and crème fraîche and serve.

CRÈME FRAÎCHE SCONES

MAKES TWELVE 2-IN/5-CM SCONES

We estimate that Sue and the other Bette's bakers have made more than a million scones since Bette's opened. It's safe to say that Sue has been around the scone block more than once. Crème fraîche makes these scones tender, moist, and tangy. If you don't have crème fraîche, you can substitute sour cream.

U.S.		METRIC
2 cups	All-purpose flour	255 g
2 tbsp	Sugar	2 tbsp
1 tbsp	Baking powder	1 tbsp
½ tsp	Sea salt	½ tsp
6 tbsp	Cold unsalted butter, cut into ½-in/12-mm pieces	85 g
3	Eggs	3
½ cup	Crème fraîche or sour cream	120 ml
2 tsp	Cool water	2 tsp
	Berry jam or lemon curd, for accompaniment	

Preheat the oven to 400°F/200°C/gas 6. Butter a baking sheet and set it aside.

Sift together the flour, sugar, baking powder, and salt into a large bowl. Using a pastry blender or two knives, cut the butter into the flour mixture until it looks to be the size of peas. Separate one of the eggs and reserve the white; in a separate bowl, whisk together the crème fraîche, the whole eggs, and the egg yolk. In a separate small bowl, mix the remaining egg white with the water and set aside. You'll use this to brush the top of each scone.

Pour the crème fraîche mixture into the flour mixture and stir lightly with a fork or a whisk until the dough just comes together. Don't overmix or your scones will be less tender.

Using a ¼-cup/60-ml measuring cup or scoop, portion the batter onto the prepared baking sheet. Brush the tops of the scones with the egg-white wash (brush lightly, you won't need all the wash). Bake until golden brown, 15 to 20 minutes.

COTTAGE CHEESE DUMPLINGS IN PARMESAN BROTH

SERVES 4; MAKES 12 TO 16 DUMPLINGS

Here is great comfort food. The texture of these dumplings is so appealing and they leave such a clean flavor in your mouth. You can also spruce up the dumplings by adding fresh herbs such as parsley, or a little finely chopped mushroom to bring out the flavor of the broth, or even saffron or a hint of curry spice. Don't add anything heavy, or it can cause the dumplings to fall apart.

U.S.		METRIC
1 cup	Whole milk cottage cheese (not low-fat)	240 ml
2	Eggs	2
½ cup	Sifted all-purpose flour	60 g
¼ tsp	Fine sea salt	¼ tsp
¼ tsp	Ground white pepper	¼ tsp
2 tbsp	Finely minced onion	2 tbsp
1 tbsp	Chopped fresh flat-leaf parsley	1 tbsp
1 tbsp	Thinly sliced fresh chives	1 tbsp
8 cups	Parmesan Broth (page 236)	2 L

In a large bowl, whisk the cottage cheese to smooth out the curd. In a separate smaller bowl, beat the eggs with a fork. Mix the beaten eggs into the cottage cheese, and then gently whisk in the flour, salt, and pepper. Gently stir in the onion and the herbs and set aside the mixture while you heat the broth.

In a 4-qt/3.8-L pot, bring the broth to a simmer. Using a soup spoon or a tablespoon, gently drop spoonful-size balls of the dumpling mixture into the simmering broth. Gently cook until the dumplings float to the surface, 5 to 8 minutes.

Spoon the cooked dumplings into four soup bowls, ladle the broth over the top, and serve while warm.

CHILLED SPRING GARLIC AND ASPARAGUS SOUP WITH CRÈME FRAÎCHE AND FRESH RICOTTA

SERVES 4

The delicate flavor of spring garlic forms the base of this soup. Choose young, tender asparagus for this: You don't purée the asparagus but slice and add it to the soup base just before serving.

To drain ricotta, gently place the cheese in a colander. Don't worry, it holds its mass and will drain.

U.S.		METRIC
3	Medium spring garlic (with bulbs and stem), halved lengthwise	3
1 tbsp	Unsalted butter	15 g
1½ cups	Peeled, diced Yukon gold potatoes	345 g
1½ cups	Diced yellow onions	345 g
3 cups	Chicken or vegetable stock	700 ml
½ cup	Crème fraîche	120 ml
12	Tender asparagus spears	12
1 cup	Fresh, drained ricotta cheese	230 g
½ tsp	Coarse sea salt	½ tsp
	Freshly ground black pepper	
1 tsp	Chopped fresh garlic chives	1 tsp

Thoroughly clean the spring garlic halves under cold running water. Dice the garlic bulb and any section of the leafy green stem that is soft and pliable. Dice as much spring garlic as needed to produce 1 cup/240 g of diced garlic.

In a medium pot with a lid, add the butter and melt over medium heat. When it's melted, add the diced garlic, potatoes, and onions. Cook in the covered pot, stirring often and covering between stirrings, until the potatoes are fork-tender and the onions are completely translucent and soft, about 8 minutes.

Add the stock to the pot, and bring the mixture to a simmer. Cook for 5 to 10 minutes, keeping the liquid at a simmer while the ingredients come together. Remove from the heat and stir in the crème fraîche. While the soup cools slightly, set up an ice bath by filling a large bowl with ice and water.

Carefully purée the soup in a blender or food processor. Pour the purée into a container, cover, and set the container in the ice bath in the refrigerator. Place four soup bowls in the refrigerator to chill.

While the soup chills, prepare the asparagus. Snap off the woody stems and blanch the spears (see Blanching Asparagus, page 240). Slice off the tip of each spear and set aside to use as a garnish. Cut the rest of each stalk crosswise into rounds. Slice the ricotta into bite-size cubes.

When the soup base is chilled, stir in the asparagus rounds and salt and season with pepper. Halve the asparagus tips lengthwise.

To serve, ladle the soup into the chilled bowls, add the ricotta cubes and asparagus tips to each bowl, and finish with a sprinkling of garlic chives.

FROMAGE BLANC SPREADS

MAKES ABOUT 1 CUP/240 ML

Fast and easy—that's the rule with these cheese spreads (pictured opposite, top to bottom: Roasted Red Pepper and Paprika, Smoked Salmon and Chives, Chocolate-Espresso, Niçoise Olive–Black Pepper, Bay Shrimp–Smoked Paprika, Roasted Garlic and Herb). They're the easiest appetizer imaginable. Set out one or two flavored spreads with crackers, crostini, or crisp vegetables such as carrot sticks, Belgian endive, and fennel. We've given a few recipes, but you really don't need to follow a recipe. Just start with about 8 ounces/230 grams of fromage blanc, then sprinkle on spices and herbs, or add diced ham and pineapple, or chopped shrimp and curry powder, or blue cheese and black pepper, or sun-dried tomatoes, or dark chocolate, or, to make the Nicoise Olive–Black Pepper spread, stir a few pitted olives into the fromage blanc and grind fresh black pepper over the top. That's really all it takes. There are a hundred ways you can go with this. We generally don't measure but just season until it tastes good. These spreads are fantastic in grilled cheese sandwiches, too.

As with any fresh cheese, the fresher it is, the better it tastes. These will keep up to 1 week in the fridge, but as they sit, the flavors will get stronger. You want to make them just before serving, if possible.

ROASTED GARLIC AND HERB SPREAD

U.S.		METRIC
8 oz	Fromage blanc	230 g
1 to 3	Large garlic cloves, roasted and cooled (see page 243)	1 to 3
1 tbsp	Finely chopped fresh flat-leaf parsley	1 tbsp
½ tsp	Finely chopped fresh tarragon	½ tsp
	Kosher salt and freshly ground black pepper	

In a bowl, mix the fromage blanc with the roasted garlic—how much roasted garlic you add is up to you; we opt for two or three large cloves, but you can add just one clove if you want a milder flavor—and the herbs. Season with salt and pepper. Serve at room temperature.

continued

FRESH TARRAGON AND GREEN GARLIC SPREAD

U.S.		METRIC
8 oz	Fromage blanc	230 g
2 to 3 tsp	Minced fresh tarragon	2 to 3 tsp
½ tsp	Minced green garlic	½ tsp

Spread the fromage blanc on a plate. With a spoon or fork, gently mix in the fresh tarragon and green garlic until evenly distributed. Serve at room temperature.

ROASTED RED PEPPER AND PAPRIKA SPREAD

U.S.		METRIC
8 oz	Fromage blanc	230 g
¼ cup	Diced roasted red pepper	45 g
⅛ tsp	Pimentón de la Vera or paprika of your choice	⅛ tsp
	A sprinkle of chopped flat-leaf parsley (optional)	

With a fork, mix the fromage blanc, roasted red pepper, pimentón, and parsley (if using) in a bowl. Serve at room temperature.

SMOKED SALMON AND CHIVES SPREAD

U.S.		METRIC
8 oz	Fromage blanc	230 g
2 tbsp	Minced smoked salmon	2 tbsp
1 tbsp	Thinly sliced fresh chives	1 tbsp

Spread the fromage blanc on a plate. With a spoon or fork, mix in the smoked salmon and fresh chives until evenly distributed. Serve at room temperature.

BAY SHRIMP–SMOKED PAPRIKA SPREAD

U.S.		METRIC
1 tbsp	Unsalted butter	1 tbsp
8 oz	Bay shrimp	230 g
½ tsp	Pimentón de la Vera	½ tsp
8 oz	Fromage blanc	230 g
	A sprinkle of chopped flat-leaf parsley	

Melt the butter in a sauté pan over medium heat. When it's done foaming, add the shrimp and cook until just pink, 2 minutes. (If your shrimp are cooked already, just warm them in the foaming butter.) Sprinkle the pimentón over the shrimp. Let cook for 10 to 20 seconds and then take the pan off the heat. Let the mixture cool and then chop the shrimp into little bits (don't chop so finely, though, that it becomes a paste).

Spread the fromage blanc on a plate. Add the shrimp-spice mixture and parsley, and, with a fork, gently toss the cheese until the shrimp is evenly distributed. Serve at room temperature.

CHOCOLATE-ESPRESSO SPREAD

U.S.		METRIC
8 oz	Fromage blanc	230 g
1-oz	Chunk of dark chocolate	30-g
Pinch	Ground espresso beans	Pinch

Spread the fromage blanc on a plate. With a microplane grater, grate the dark chocolate over the cheese. Sprinkle the ground espresso beans on top. With a spoon or fork, gently toss the cheese until the mixture is nicely speckled. Serve at room temperature.

RICOTTA-ASPARAGUS SOUFFLÉ

SERVES 8

This soufflé is light, satisfying, and beautiful. You can envision a French farmwife from the last century making this, and it's a bit wondrous that we make it much the same way today, and take such pleasure in this technique. Very flavorful but still cloud-like, this soufflé is light enough for a warm summer's day. For a richer version, see the Sweet Smokey Blue and Bacon Soufflé (page 195).

Use a good ricotta—we like Bellwether Farms' Whole Milk Ricotta. And the eggs need to be fresh, or the whites won't get as fluffy as they need to be.

Béchamel

U.S.		METRIC
1 cup	Whole milk or half-and-half	240 ml
4	Egg yolks	4
2 tbsp	Unsalted butter	2 tbsp
2 tbsp	All-purpose flour	2 tbsp
1 tbsp	Thinly sliced fresh chives	1 tbsp
½ cup	Ricotta cheese	125 g
¼ tsp	Sea salt	¼ tsp
⅛ tsp	Freshly ground black pepper	⅛ tsp

Soufflé

U.S.		METRIC
6	Fat asparagus spears, blanched (see page 240)	6
4	Egg whites	4
2 tsp	Finely chopped fresh basil	2 tsp
2 tsp	Finely chopped fresh chives	2 tsp
2 tsp	Chopped fresh flat-leaf parsley	2 tsp

Butter a 10-in/25-cm baking dish and set it aside.

To make the béchamel: Whisk together the milk and egg yolks and set aside. Add the butter to a medium saucepan or skillet (don't use a nonstick pan). When it's sizzling, add the flour and whisk constantly over medium heat until the mixture shows just a little color. Don't let it turn brown. Keep whisking while you slowly pour in the milk-egg mixture. It's fine if the butter and flour seize up when you add the liquid. Just keep whisking. Add the chives and, while whisking, let the mixture cook over

continued

medium heat until it thickens slightly, about 1 minute. When the mixture has a velvety texture, stir in the ricotta, salt, and pepper. Set the mixture in the pan aside to cool to room temperature (so the eggs won't curdle when you add the warm, blanched asparagus).

To make the soufflé: Preheat the oven to 450°F/230°C/gas 8.

Cut the blanched asparagus stalks into thin rounds all the way up to and including the tip of each spear. Set aside. With an electric mixer on medium-high speed or with a whisk, whip the egg whites until they hold a gentle peak. Don't overbeat, or you'll break the proteins and the whites won't expand as much during cooking. Gently fold the basil and chives into the beaten whites.

Touch the béchamel to be sure it's at room temperature. Stir the asparagus into the cooled béchamel. Gently fold in about half of the egg whites. Very delicately fold in the last of the egg whites and pour the mixture into the buttered pan.

Cook the soufflé for 7 minutes and then decrease the heat to 400°F/200°C/gas 6. Cook until the soufflé is lightly browned on top and a skewer inserted in the center comes out clean, 10 to 12 minutes more.

Sprinkle the parsley over the top and serve right away.

CORN VARIATION:
If you can find both good sweet corn and tender asparagus at the same time, this soufflé is even better if you add about 1 cup/175 g corn kernels when you add the asparagus. Don't bother measuring. Just cut all the kernels off one large ear of perfect corn. You don't need to cook the ear or the kernels beforehand. The raw kernels will cook perfectly while the soufflé bakes.

LEMON-GINGER CRÈME FRAÎCHE GRANITA

SERVES 6 TO 8

Tangy, creamy, and yet still light, this granita doesn't require an ice-cream machine. You just need a stainless-steel pan or liner and a fork to scrape up the ice crystals every hour or so. A glass container will work as well, although liquid freezes faster in stainless steel. A pan that measures 9 by 9 in/23 by 23 cm or 13 by 9 in/33 by 23 cm is large enough so the liquid is relatively shallow.

Use Meyer lemons for this if you can get them, but it's good made with any juicy lemon.

U.S.		METRIC
¼ cup	Freshly squeezed lemon juice	60 ml
1 tsp	Finely minced lemon zest	1 tsp
1 tsp	Finely minced candied ginger	1 tsp
¼ cup	Sugar	50 g
1 cup	Crème fraîche	240 ml
1 cup	Milk (whole or low-fat)	240 ml
2	Big whole stems of basil	2

Combine the lemon juice, lemon zest, candied ginger, and sugar in a medium saucepan over medium heat. Bring to a simmer and let it cook for about 2 minutes. Taste the liquid. The heat will neutralize the lemon's acidity so the juice doesn't taste so puckery and so it doesn't curdle the milk. Pour in the crème fraîche and milk. Rub the whole basil stems between your hands to release the oils and add them to the mixture. Let steep in the warm liquid until completely cool.

Remove the basil from the liquid and discard. Pour the liquid into a shallow stainless-steel pan, cover well with plastic wrap, and place it in the freezer. After 45 minutes to 1 hour, use a fork to scrape up the frozen crystals. Replace the plastic wrap and put the pan back in the freezer. An hour later, scrape again. Do this four times, and then spoon the granita into small bowls to serve or cover well with plastic wrap and store in the freezer. Fluff the granita with a fork just before serving. This delicate frozen dessert is best served the day you make it.

THE COWGIRLS' INTERPRETATION OF
ELLEN STRAUS'S CHEESECAKE

SERVES 8 TO 10

We'd like to say this is Ellen Straus's cheesecake, famous throughout Point Reyes, but we can't. Ellen's cheesecake was top secret. Every Friday, Ellen would come to our barn and make fresh quark, fromage blanc, and crème fraîche with Sue. When they finished, Ellen potted up a few tubs of the very fresh cheeses and carried them over to the kitchen on the other side of the building where Peggy would be working.

When Ellen made her cheesecake, she went to great lengths to be sure nobody was watching. She wanted her recipe saved for her daughters and insisted her recipe be kept secret. Every time she made this, she would position herself at the table by the ovens, facing the wall with her back to the door, making sure that nobody could see exactly what she was doing.

As consistently delicious as it was, Ellen never used the same combination of cheeses. The first few times she used all quark, and the texture was loose and the flavor flat. Then Peggy noticed that she added more lemon the next time and lots of crème fraîche. After that Ellen used fromage blanc instead of quark.

Although we cannot claim that this is Ellen's recipe exactly, we make it with her in mind and like to think we are continuing her spirit of improvisation.

Shortbread Crust

U.S.		METRIC
1¼ cups	All-purpose flour	150 g
¼ cup	Sugar	50 g
1 tsp	Freshly grated lemon zest	1 tsp
¼ tsp	Kosher salt	¼ tsp
½ cup	Chilled unsalted butter, cubed	115 g
1	Egg yolk	1
½ tsp	Pure vanilla extract	½ tsp

Filling

U.S.		METRIC
2 cups	Fromage blanc	460 g
1 cup	Crème fraîche	240 ml
½ cup	Sugar	100 g
1 tbsp	Freshly grated lemon zest	1 tbsp
2 tbsp	Freshly squeezed lemon juice	2 tbsp
1 tbsp	Pure vanilla extract	1 tbsp
2	Egg yolks	2

To make the crust: Butter and flour a 9-in/23-cm or 10-in/25-cm springform pan, and set it aside. Add the flour, sugar, lemon zest, salt, butter, egg yolk, and vanilla to the bowl of a stand mixer fitted with the paddle attachment. Mix at medium speed until the dough is thoroughly combined (or combine with a handheld electric mixer). Press the dough into the bottom of the prepared pan and, with your fingers, work it so it goes a quarter of the way up the sides of the pan. Refrigerate for 30 minutes.

Preheat the oven to 375°F/190°C/gas 5. Bake the crust until golden (don't let it darken), about 15 minutes. Let the crust cool while you prepare the filling.

To make the filling: Decrease the oven temperature to 350°F/180°C/gas 4. In the bowl of a stand mixer fitted with the paddle attachment (or with a handheld electric mixer), beat the fromage blanc and crème fraîche on medium-low speed until smooth. Add the sugar a few spoonfuls at a time. When all the sugar has been incorporated, add the lemon zest, lemon juice, vanilla, and egg yolks.

Pour the filling into the crust and bake until the top is slightly brown and the filling begins to pull away from the sides, about 1 hour. Remove the cheesecake from the oven, and let it cool for an hour in the pan.

When ready to serve, loosen the pan and remove the cake. Run a knife between the crust and the bottom of the pan, then transfer the cheesecake to a platter. Cut into slices using a long length of clean dental floss or a sharp knife.

SOFT, YOUNG AGED CHEESES

THERE IS SOMETHING VERY AMERICAN about cheeses that don't follow a proven formula. European cheesemakers put a lot of stock in centuries-old methods, and we depend on those trusted techniques as we develop new cheeses. But there's also a lot to be said for the pioneers who step away from tradition.

American cheesemakers feel more free to experiment than our European cheesemaking friends because we know that if we come up with a delicious cheese, even if it's untraditional, it can be accepted and even welcomed. Every week we get to try the results of innovative experiments in cheesemaking; it's one of the best parts of our job. We're excited to taste the work of a cheesemaker in Vermont who starts with a recipe for a mountain tomme and then grows a white mold on the rind, or a cheesemaker in California who starts with a basic tomme recipe and then inoculates the milk with blue mold and pierces the center with long needles to create a layer of blue.

Although we took an unconventional path in developing Mt Tam, eventually that path led to the cheese we'd hoped for.

OUR FOURTH CHEESE: MT TAM, OUR FIRST AGED CHEESE

Things were humming along nicely in our creamery as we turned out fromage blanc, quark, and crème fraîche, as well as a beautiful batch of cottage cheese every Tuesday. Ready for more of a challenge, we set out to make our first aged cheese, and imagined presenting it to restaurant chefs for use in a cheese course. We thought about the type of cheeses we wanted to make. Saint André appealed to us because it seemed accessible. Even people who knew little about cheese liked this deliciously creamy French import. More important, Saint André has a luscious texture that highlighted the milk's flavors, and that's what we aimed to do: make a cheese that enhanced the delicious flavors in Straus milk.

Just as we were preparing to make our first complex cheese, Fons Smits approached us at our stall at a San Francisco farmers' market, asking if we had any jobs. Fons had a degree in dairy science in Holland, his native country, and some experience training cheesemakers. As neither of us had a science background, we welcomed a person who did, and we hired him on the spot.

When Fons had worked with Sue for a short time making our cheeses, the two of them set out to make a new aged cheese. Being from the Netherlands, Fons had experience making Dutch Gouda-style cheeses but no background making the kind of cheese we had in mind. So, we started with a Gouda recipe, and with every batch we shifted the technique just slightly, aiming for a cheese that came closer to the creamy texture we were envisioning.

When making a classic Gouda, the milk is heated, lactic acid cultures are added, and, a short while later, rennet is introduced to the mix. The addition of rennet encourages the proteins in the milk to knit together, forming a sturdy curd.

The curd is cut into small cubes and stirred until the mixture resembles cottage cheese curd. Some of the whey is then drained off and hot water is poured over the curds, which coaxes out a little more whey. The liquid is again drained off and the curd is then scooped into molds that are stacked, pressed under heavy weights, and allowed to drain overnight. The cheese comes out of the molds in the morning and is brined in a strong salt solution before being wheeled to the aging room.

Mt Tam is made with a cooked and washed curd, just like the classic Gouda. Rennet is the primary coagulant in our cheese, and lactic acid cultures contribute tangy, buttery flavors that slowly emerge as the cheese ages, just as with true Gouda.

Up until this point, we're following the Gouda process, but here's where we switch paths. We enrich the milk by adding cream, which isn't done with Goudas. We pasteurize, and then inoculate with *Penicillium candidum* (not a Gouda tradition) and cultures. Vegetarian rennet is added after the cultures have a chance to activate in the vat. The milk sets within an hour and the curd is then cut into cubes and allowed to form a thin skin. The curds are then stirred, softly and slowly, for about an hour (Gouda is stirred more vigorously).

When the curds are firm and tight, some whey is drained from the vat. Warm water is poured over the remaining curds, cooking them slightly and allowing more whey to be released (Gouda would be cooked at a higher temperature and stirred assertively once more). The curds are stirred and then ladled into small cheese forms or hoops, turned, allowed to drain overnight, then brined in the morning, and never pressed under heavy weights, as Gouda is.

By following the example of French cheesemakers, who rely on lactic acid for fermentation, flavor, and coagulation, and combining these techniques with Dutch methods of washing the curds in hot water and using rennet for coagulation, we were able to create a new variety of cheese. We called it Mt Tam after the iconic peak at the northern foot of the Golden Gate Bridge.

In retrospect, given the type of cheese we had in mind, we probably shouldn't have started with a Gouda recipe, but some of our favorite aspects of Mt Tam come from this unorthodox pairing of Dutch and French cheesemaking methods.

After Fons left, we worked hard to improve Mt Tam. In 2001, when Maureen Cunnie joined our cheesemaking team, she continued to improve the recipe. Maureen had cooked with long-time chef Annie Somerville at Greens restaurant in San Francisco. She understood immediately what we were aiming for in our cheesemaking. She added more cream, cooked the curds at a lower temperature, and helped finesse the cheese's rind development.

Mt Tam continues to be the most popular of all our cheeses. As of this writing, even though we make more than a dozen cheeses, Mt Tam accounts for a good portion of our sales, and Maureen Cunnie still leads our cheesemaking operation. (That's Maureen on page 81.)

Another way in which Cowgirl Creamery stepped away from tradition is in showing folks who visit us how we make our cheeses. In the early years, our goal was to make excellent fresh cheeses similar to the cheeses made by Neal's Yard Dairy, but we wanted our cheeses to highlight the unique flavors of the milk sourced exclusively from the Straus dairy.

We adopted the Neal's Yard model when designing our cheesemaking room in Point Reyes, but instead of making cheese off-site as Neal's Yard Dairy does, we made it in a glassed-in room near the entrance to our barn. This concept followed the restaurant philosophy that both of us had embraced during our years in Berkeley. Chez Panisse and Bette's Diner were early adapters of an "open kitchen" layout where the cooking takes place in the dining room, not in some mysterious, off-limits space hidden behind a swinging metal door. We wanted the same ambiance at our Point Reyes creamery; we felt that our customers might enjoy seeing how we made our cheeses. In essence, we built an "open creamery" in Point Reyes, sealed behind a glass wall.

There are two reasons for that glass wall. One is hygiene. We want customers to see our cheeses but want our cheese rooms closed and pristinely clean and white. The other reason is molds and bacteria. Molds, which are crucial to a cheese's aging process, are delicate, moving easily through the air. Cheesemakers have worked hard to isolate the beneficial molds inside the aging room, and don't want the addition of competing molds and bacteria.

By slightly altering the balance of molds, yeasts, and cultures, cheesemakers can help determine the flavors that soft aged cheeses develop as they age.

Because both of our soft aged cheeses, Mt Tam and Red Hawk, are hybrid cheeses, we never know how to enter them in competitions. They are neither Gouda nor Camembert, though the first half of the process for making both Mt Tam and Red Hawk comes from Gouda-style cheesemaking methods, while later steps more closely resemble a recipe for Camembert. When the head judge of one cheese competition suggested that we enter Mt Tam and Red Hawk in a category called American Originals, that made sense to us.

Mary Keehn is another cheesemaker whose cheese, Humboldt Fog, qualifies for this American Originals category. When Mary developed her soft aged goat milk cheese, she added another element that made sense to her: a layer of vegetable ash that ran through the cheese's center. Although Morbier, a cow milk cheese from France, shows a layer of ash in the center, this wasn't something you ever saw in a goat milk cheese. Mary created a true American original.

Red Hawk falls into this category because it's a triple-crème cheese with a washed rind. The terms "double-crème" and "triple-crème" refer to the butterfat content of a cheese. If a cheese's butterfat content measures between 60 percent and 74 percent, the cheese is labeled double-crème. If the butterfat content is 75 percent or more, the cheese is a triple-crème. Washing the rind of triple-crème cheese is not a traditional technique and is considered difficult due to potential development of off flavors from high levels of butterfat.

OUR FIFTH CHEESE: RED HAWK, OUR FIRST WASHED-RIND CHEESE

Red Hawk is the best mistake we've ever made. Sue made the first batch of Red Hawk while trying to correct a flaw on the rind of a Mt Tam. Ordinarily, Mt Tam begins to develop a nice, fluffy, white *Penicillium candidum* fuzz within four or five days. When Sue went to turn the cheese, it was bald and mottled. She looked more closely and found that cheese mites had jumped off the Stilton that was also in the aging room, had landed on Mt Tam, and were inhibiting the mold's growth.

Sue re-inoculated the rind by spraying it with a solution of *candidum* mold and water, but instead of encouraging the bloomy growth, the treatment killed the mold, allowing wild *B. linens* to take over. *B. linens* is a beneficial bacterium often found on cheese rinds. This rind was a light pink color and sticky to the touch. Sue was so upset that she plopped the cheese on the bottom rack, walked off, and promptly forgot all about it.

Three weeks later, Kate Arding, who had come from Neal's Yard Dairy to help us set up "a proper cheese counter" (you may want to say that out loud with a British accent), discovered the cheese Sue had abandoned. The cheese had continued to ripen and develop strong aromas. Kate cut open one of the cheeses, marveled at the gooey texture, and tasted it. Kate was so excited she ran out of the aging room to find us. "This is the best cheese you've ever made," she told us. "It's rich and savory, almost meaty in flavor with perhaps a hint of anchovies and lemon. It has such a long, sweet-cream finish. Can you do it again?"

After much discussion, tasting, and research, we realized that we had inadvertently created a washed-rind cheese with an aroma that was almost alarmingly strong but with flavors that were seductively mellow. The *B. linens* is the dominant bacterium that cheesemakers use to wash the rinds of big-flavored cheeses such as Taleggio and Vacherin. This family of molds thrives in cool, humid climates and grows even faster when salt is introduced, so the Point Reyes environment is ideal for the cultivation of these bacteria. While most cheesemakers have to inoculate the rind with *B. linens,* we don't need to. Where we live it's wild and grows everywhere, so over time we were able to replicate our mistake.

In 2003, Red Hawk was judged the Best of Show at the annual American Cheese Society competition. It was the first time a washed-rind cheese had ever won the contest.

MOLDS AND THE AGING PROCESS

Cheesemakers rely on naturally occurring molds (as we rely on the *B. linens* that changed the flavors found in Mt Tam to the flavors present in Red Hawk) as well as molds that are introduced during the cheesemaking process. The *Penicillium candidum* develops as the rind is exposed to air; the fluffy white mold coats the dark grey ash on Humboldt Fog, for example, to make a beautiful mottled design. Multiple variations in shape and rind treatment make this one of the largest and most creative cheese categories.

Some cheesemakers introduce *Geotrichum* yeast in the vat along with *Penicillium candidum* mold, which both grow on the rind in the aging room, creating a dense prune-like rind texture and a deep, yeasty flavor. Crottin cheese, made with goat milk, best demonstrates this style of cheesemaking. It is made with a fresh chèvre, just like Mary's Humboldt Fog, except it is pressed into tiny cylindrical forms, drained again, then salted. No ash is added, so the rind becomes a pale yellow with a dusting of white mold.

COWGIRL SEASONAL CHEESES:
EXPERIMENTING WITH MILK FROM A DIFFERENT HERD

For our first twelve years of cheesemaking, we worked exclusively with milk delivered directly to our two creameries from Albert Straus's dairy. Albert was expanding his production of bottled milk, butter, and yogurt and for that purpose had begun sourcing milk from other organic dairies in our area. It seemed every dairy in Sonoma and Marin was transitioning to organic. At one point in 2008, so many dairies had transitioned that there was a glut in the market that was exacerbated by the global financial meltdown that same year.

During that time we got a call from John Taverna, whose small dairy in the Chileno Valley, near Petaluma, was newly certified as organic. John was desperate to find a buyer for his dairy's milk from his Jersey herd. We put our heads together and came up with the idea of making a seasonal cheese with his extra rich, buttery milk. With each new season we could design a new rind treatment, and we'd get to experiment to find which rind best highlighted the subtle changes in the milk flavors from season to season.

Our commitment to purchase milk from the Taverna dairy gave John one sale he could be sure of, and it gave us a reason to step outside our comfort zone and work with a milk that was totally different from the Straus milk that we'd come to know so well.

All our seasonal cheeses begin with our recipe for Mt Tam, but we don't add cream, and we change rind treatments and additions to suit each season. You can taste any of these cheeses beside Mt Tam to see how just changing milk from one dairy to another changes a cheese's character.

St Pat

Our spring cheese, St Pat, has a hardier texture, which allows us to mature the cheese in the aging room longer than we can age Mt Tam. We inoculate the milk with *Penicillium candidum*, so white mold is evident on the rind. After the cheese is hooped and brined, it is wrapped in stinging nettle leaves harvested from a local, organic farm. We call it St Pat because the nettles start to appear along the creek beds in February, which means the cheese can be ready for release on St. Patrick's Day.

Pierce Pt

During the summer, John's cows eat lots of fresh grass, which makes their milk bright and full of life. We ask farmer Janet Brown of Allstar Organics Farm to harvest and dry wildflowers and herbs. Used on the rind of Pierce Pt, these highlight the pastoral flavors of the cheese. Pierce Point is the very tip of the peninsula. A walk there in the summer surrounds you with the fragrance of calendula, basil, chamomile, and field flowers, the flavors found in this cheese.

Chimney Rock

We were walking past the Far West Fungi shop at the Ferry Building one day while the shop was featuring an organic pioppini mushroom with deep, earthy notes. We realized this would be the ideal addition to the rind of an autumn cheese. At the creamery, Maureen and Peggy combined pioppini mushrooms with savory herbs and pepper and added a little shiitake mushroom powder for an even bigger mushroom flavor, and our fall cheese was born. During the fall, John gives his cows alfalfa and hay in addition to their normal grass diet; the mushroom flavors highlight these changes in the milk.

Devil's Gulch

Cheese made with winter milk generally has milder flavors than spring or summer, which makes winter cheese a good candidate for a little spice. Again, we looked to Janet Brown of Allstar Organics Farm, who grows vibrant spicy and sweet peppers on a parcel of land in Petaluma. Janet oven-dries the peppers and delivers them right to our creamery. Devil's Gulch, named after a narrow ravine carved along the base of Mount Barnaby and just down the road from Janet's farm, packs a visual punch, with its bright, red pepper–flecked rind. This cheese has the biggest spice kick of any of our cheeses.

Our weekly tasting of soon-to-be released Cowgirl Creamery cheeses.

TOMATO-WATERMELON PANZANELLA SALAD WITH FETA

SERVES 8 TO 10

When you have ripe summer tomatoes, sweet and juicy watermelon, and leftover good bread, this flavorful bread salad makes the most of them. Day-old bread works best. We tend to see how much bread we have left over and work from there. Whether you have a handful of bread cubes, or several, this recipe works as long as you toss in the same amount of watermelon or tomato. It's also a good idea to cut the bread, watermelon, and tomatoes into chunks of similar size.

You can make this with just tomatoes and bread (a 2:1 ratio) or just watermelon and bread, but the combination of melon, tomatoes, and bread tastes best because of the contrasting flavors. Use whichever tomato smells and looks the best at your farmers' market; a combination of heirloom and halved cherry tomatoes works well.

Don't add the feta until you've already added the bread and tossed it. If you don't have feta, ricotta works well in this salad, too.

On a hot day, we serve this with grilled flank steak for a hearty, yet refreshing meal.

U.S.		METRIC
1	Garlic clove, halved	1
½-lb	Loaf levain or any good country-style bread	225-g
4 tbsp	Extra-virgin olive oil	60 ml
1 tbsp	Coarse sea salt	1 tbsp
1 tbsp	Champagne vinegar	1 tbsp
1 tbsp	Balsamic vinegar	1 tbsp
2	Shallots, minced	2
Pinch	Freshly ground black pepper	Pinch
3 cups	Quartered tomatoes	3 cups
3 cups	Cubed watermelon	3 cups
3 tbsp	Fresh basil chiffonade (see page 243)	3 tbsp
8 oz	Feta cheese or ricotta salata	230 g
1	Head red romaine or butter lettuce or other greens	1

Preheat the oven to 350°F/180°C/gas 4 and (on a hot day as it was when we photographed this) set salad plates in the refrigerator to chill.

continued

Rub the cut side of the garlic clove all over the bread's crust, and then cut the bread into slices that are ¾ in/2 cm thick. Cut the slices into cubes. (You should have about 3 cups of bread cubes. If you have more, that's fine. Just increase the amount of tomato and watermelon to match the bread measure.) Spread the bread cubes on an ungreased baking sheet. Drizzle 2 tbsp of the olive oil over the bread cubes and sprinkle them with 1 tsp of the salt. Bake until the bread has hard corners, but still has some squish inside, about 10 minutes. (Don't let the bread turn dark, but let it get hard enough so it doesn't turn to mush when you mix the panzanella together.)

While the bread toasts, pour both vinegars over the shallots in a small bowl. Add 1 tsp salt and the pepper, stir, and then set the bowl aside to let the shallots macerate in the vinegar.

Toss the tomato and watermelon in a large bowl and sprinkle on the remaining 1 tsp salt. When the bread cubes are toasted, toss them into the bowl with the tomatoes and watermelon. Whisk 2 tbsp of the basil chiffonade and the remaining 2 tbsp olive oil into the vinegar and shallots and pour over the bread and fruit, scraping all the shallot and basil bits into the salad. Gently toss the salad. Coarsely chop the feta into shards. Don't worry too much about size. When the basil is evenly distributed, add the feta, gently tossing so the cheese doesn't break up too much.

Arrange lettuce around the platter as a garnish. Finish with a sprinkle of basil chiffonade before serving.

FETA AND CUCUMBER SALAD
SERVES 4

A true Greek salad is all about the feta, which makes this salad a good way to taste fetas and see which you like. Start with a classic feta from Greece, then try some of the good fetas from Bulgaria, and compare to the sheep and goat milk fetas coming out of California. A feta-tasting party with several kinds of feta, and simple Greek salads made from each cheese, can help shine a light on which fetas you most enjoy.

Cucumbers, feta, thinly sliced onion, and kalamata olives, as well as a fruity olive oil and fresh lemon juice are really all you need. You can also treat this salad as a starting point and add tomatoes when they're at their peak or thin strips of bright red bell pepper. When we put this on the menu at our Cowgirl Cantina in Point Reyes, it sells out as fast as we can make it.

U.S.		METRIC
2	Large cucumbers	2
8 oz	Feta cheese	230 g
12	Kalamata olives, pitted and halved	12
½	Red onion, thinly sliced	½
⅓ cup	Fruity extra-virgin olive oil	75 ml
1 tbsp	Fresh mint chiffonade (see page 243)	1 tbsp
	Squeeze of fresh lemon juice	
	Sea salt and freshly ground black pepper	

SEASONAL ADDITIONS (TO ADD AS YOU LIKE)

U.S.		METRIC
¼ cup	Julienned red bell pepper	50 g
½ cup	Fresh tomato chunks	100 g
½ cup	Chunks of peeled jicama	100 g

Peel the cucumbers, halve lengthwise, and then slice into half-moons about 1 in/2.5 cm thick. In a large bowl, mix the cucumber slices, feta, olives, onion, and olive oil. Toss in the mint and season with lemon juice, salt, and pepper. Stir and taste to see if you'd like more lemon juice, salt, or pepper. Add the red bell pepper, tomato, jicama, or any other vegetable you like.

This keeps in the refrigerator for up to 1 week. We like it best after it's been sitting in the fridge and marinating for a few days.

WINTER SALAD GREENS WITH PERSIMMON VINAIGRETTE AND MT TAM

SERVES 4

If you have beautiful lettuce that you've grown yourself or found in a farmers' market, this might be the recipe to use. When Peggy finds exceptional lettuce, she thinks of Jean-Pierre Moullé, the chef at Chez Panisse, as well as our good friend Todd Koons.

A classically trained French chef, Jean-Pierre Moullé is a thoughtful, caring cook who shares his knowledge generously. His influence on a generation of cooks is far-reaching; many people who cook today have adopted his cooking style. The cooks who worked with Jean-Pierre perhaps loved best that Jean-Pierre always gave you (or his cooking) his entire attention and welcomed questions.

Jean-Pierre is an accomplished hunter and fisherman, but Peggy associates him with lettuce because of the delicate lettuces he harvested from his tiny garden in Berkeley. Peggy viewed it as an honor and a privilege when Jean-Pierre asked her to care for his garden while he went on vacation.

Jean-Pierre brought all of his lettuces to Chez Panisse; Todd Koons, at the age of nineteen, realized that California restaurants would buy many of the specialty lettuces that weren't available in the United States at that time (unless you knew Jean-Pierre). Todd helped bring organic, field-grown heirloom lettuces to a wider market.

Jean-Pierre has changed much more than the type of lettuce we find in restaurants today. Peggy speaks for many cooks when she expresses gratitude for the many lessons Jean-Pierre taught—most important, always spend the time needed to do a task well and always appreciate the food on the plate, the wine in the glass, and the people around you.

Persimmon Vinaigrette

U.S.		METRIC
3 tbsp	Champagne vinegar	3 tbsp
1	Small shallot, minced	1
½	Ripe Fuyu persimmon, peeled, seeded, and finely chopped, juices reserved	½
¼ cup	Extra-virgin olive oil	60 ml
	Fine sea salt and freshly ground black pepper	
3 cups	Fresh, beautiful greens (any combination of radicchio, speckled lettuce, Belgian endive, or escarole), washed and torn into pieces	720 ml

continued

½	Ripe Fuyu persimmon, peeled, seeded, and chopped	½
4 slices	Levain bread, cut slightly on the diagonal	4 slices
4 tbsp	Mt Tam cheese (paste only, not the rind)	60 ml

To make the vinaigrette: In a small bowl, pour the vinegar over the shallot. Let it sit for 10 minutes.

Whisk together the finely chopped persimmon and any juice with the shallot and Champagne vinegar. Whisk in the olive oil slowly, and continue whisking until it emulsifies. Add ¼ tsp salt and a few grinds of pepper, taste the vinaigrette, and decide if you'd like more salt and pepper.

When you're just about ready to serve, dress the salad greens with the vinaigrette. Spoon one-fourth of the dressed greens onto four salad plates and top with the persimmon chunks.

Very lightly toast the bread slices. You want them to be warm but still tender and not overly crisp. Spread 1 tbsp of Mt Tam on each warm bread slice, set it on the plate beside the salad, and serve.

CAMEMBERT OR BRIE LAYERED WITH TRUFFLES OR WILD MUSHROOMS

SERVES 8 TO 10 AS AN APPETIZER

When Pascale Cazalas of Jean d'Alos Fromager in Bordeaux first made this creation for us, she was careful to do it behind closed doors. In Berkeley for French Cheese Week at Chez Panisse, Pascale assembled this special cheese in her room at the B&B where she was staying rather than risk having anyone see how she made it. Luckily, Peggy, who has keen recipe-cracking skills, experimented and devised her own formula for this delicacy.

Even though Pascale speaks little English and Peggy speaks little French, they have become great friends over the years. This Camembert recipe reminds Peggy of the first time Pascale addressed the staff at Chez Panisse. The restaurant was closed on Sunday afternoons, when the staff often got together to hear speakers or meet purveyors. Pascale gave a talk about women cheesemakers throughout history, how the men managed the herd while the women cared for the cheeses and handed down these skills.

Pascale had never spoken in front of an audience, and she was afraid that she wouldn't be able to adequately convey her thoughts in English on this topic, which meant so much to her. Everyone in the room listened intently, perched on the edge of their seats. When she had finished speaking, and her listeners spontaneously applauded, Pascale broke into tears. She was so pleased that her message was understood and appreciated.

Every year or so, Peggy goes to Bordeaux to visit Pascale and Jean-Claude, and even though Pascale's English has not improved all that much and Peggy's French has not yet reached fluency, they seem to communicate without any trouble at all.

We like that both Pascale and Peggy make this cheese during the winter holidays, Pascale in France and Peggy in California. It's a very special way to make your Camembert or Brie very festive and memorable.

After slicing the cheese in half horizontally, from side to side, and layering on the the mushrooms, you reassemble it, wrap the cheese tightly, and put it back in your refrigerator to let the mold form and seal the edges back up. You'll want to make this at least three days before you plan to serve it, and seven days in advance is even better. If you plan to let it sit for seven days, buy a slightly underripe cheese and place it in the coldest section of your refrigerator.

If using wild mushrooms, sauté them in butter and let them cool before you slice the cheese. If using truffles, just shave them over the cheese once you've sliced it open.

continued

U.S.		METRIC
1	Whole Camembert, Brie, or Cameo cheese	1
	Shaved truffle or	
½ cup	Thinly sliced wild mushrooms (such as chanterelles), sautéed in 1 tbsp butter	85 g
	Slices of a very good baguette or levain bread, for accompaniment	

Halve the cheese horizontally, from side to side, as if you were slicing a bagel. Pay attention to how you separate the two halves, as you'll want to put them back together so all the edges align again.

With a knife, scrape a little cheese from the inside of each half to make room for the filling. (Eat those scrapings on crackers or bread, if you like.)

Add the truffle or wild mushrooms directly to the cut side of one half of the cheese. We don't measure the truffle, but just shave it right over the open face of the cheese. If pushed, we'd say about 1 tbsp, but just shave until the surface has a light layer of truffle all the way across. Carefully reassemble the cheese, cut-sides facing, matching it up as best as you can. Cover the cheese with plastic wrap, smoothing it down so there's no bit of the cheese exposed to air. Refrigerate for at least 3 days or up to 7 days.

On the day you plan to serve it, let it come to room temperature, setting it out about 3 hours beforehand.

Serve with slices of very good baguettes or levain.

CROOKNECK SQUASH AND CORN SOUP
WITH HUMBOLDT FOG

SERVES 6

This is our good friend Peg Janosch's go-to recipe for drop-in guests. Peg has been our go-to person concerning finance and business development from the beginning.

This bright, velvety soup forms a mellow backdrop to elegant, luscious Humboldt Fog. We love this method of placing a single slice of cheese on top of a warm bowl of soup just before serving.

Make the soup ahead if you like but don't add the cheese to the hot soup until you've ladled the soup into bowls and are ready to eat.

U.S.		METRIC
3	Large crookneck squash	3
4 cups	Parmesan Broth (page 236) or store-bought vegetable or chicken stock	960 ml
1 tbsp plus 2 tsp	Unsalted butter	1 tbsp plus 2 tsp
1 tbsp	Extra-virgin olive oil	1 tbsp
1½ cups	Diced yellow onion	225 g
2	Garlic cloves, minced	2
½ cup	Raw corn kernels (from 1 ear of corn)	90 g
3 oz	Humboldt Fog cheese	85 g
2 tbsp	Baby basil leaves or basil chiffonade (see page 243)	2 tbsp

Cut the squash into chunks that are 1 in/2.5 cm. Reserve a few squash chunks and cut them into fine pieces. Set the chunks and the pieces aside. Pour the broth into a large pot over medium-high heat.

In a separate large soup pot, heat the 1 tbsp butter and olive oil. When the butter is melted, add the onion and cook over medium heat. (Decrease the heat to medium-low and give it a few more minutes if you're not standing over the pot.) After a few minutes, add the garlic. Cook until the onion is translucent, about 10 minutes. Ladle in the warm stock, and add the bigger chunks of squash. Don't add the finely chopped squash yet.

continued

Simmer until the squash is tender when pierced with a knife, about 20 minutes. Take the pot off the heat, let cool for at least 30 minutes, and then purée the squash mixture in a blender or food processor. Push the puréed mixture through a medium-mesh strainer. (Don't use a fine-mesh strainer, or the soup will be too thin.) At this point you can continue making the soup or refrigerate the soup (and don't forget to tightly wrap up and refrigerate the reserved finely chopped squash).

When ready to serve the soup, pour it into a pan over medium-low heat. In a skillet, melt the 2 tsp butter. Add the reserved finely chopped squash and the corn kernels, and sauté, stirring constantly, just until the squash and corn are heated. Take the skillet off the heat.

Slice the cheese into six even pieces, and cut the rind from each piece. Discard the rinds.

When the soup is hot, stir in the corn and squash bits.

Ladle the soup into six bowls. Float one cheese slice into the center of each bowl of soup and top with baby basil leaves.

CHEF'S NOTE:
If you warm the stock before you pour it into the soup, the final texture will be better. Pouring cold stock into a hot pan causes a film of butter and oil to rise to the top of the soup.

For a creamier soup, stir 2 tbsp crème fraîche into each bowl of soup before you add the cheese and basil.

For a spicier version of this soup, stir in a few tbsp of the Roasted Red Pepper and Paprika Spread on page 112.

GOUGÈRES

MAKES 48 CHEESE PUFFS

There's a kind of magic to a gougère, the way the cream puff dough puffs during baking and forms a hollow center. You can fill these with a savory herbed fromage blanc or with rich mascarpone cheese mixed with chocolate. We like to pile these high on a platter as part of a cheese board and buffet. They also make an elegant nibble with Champagne.

Gruyère makes these gougères tender and flavorful. You could substitute Comté or Emmenthaler or Pleasant Ridge Reserve—any grated Alpine-style cheese works well.

Choux Paste

U.S.		METRIC
½ cup	Water	120 ml
½ cup	Milk	120 ml
½ cup	Unsalted butter, cut into small pieces	115 g
½ tsp	Sea salt	½ tsp
1 cup	All-purpose flour	125 g
4 oz	Gruyère cheese, grated	115 g
4	Eggs	4

Fillings

Fromage Blanc Spreads (page 111)

Dark Chocolate Filling (recipe follows)

Preheat the oven to 400°F/200°C/gas 6. Butter a baking sheet (two, if you have another).

To make the choux paste: In a medium saucepan, heat the water, milk, butter, and salt. While the mixture heats, sift the flour into a large heatproof bowl. When the liquid comes to a boil, pour it over the flour and stir until combined. Stir in the cheese gradually with a wooden spoon, and give the mix at least 10 or 15 minutes to cool. Stir in the eggs one at a time.

Spoon the batter into a cone that you've made out of stiff paper (see page 243) or a resealable plastic bag (snip off the corner after filling). To form the gougère, squeeze out the batter onto the prepared baking sheet into mounds the size of an egg. As you squeeze out batter, push the tip of the cone into the center of the mound and then lift, forming a peak on each gougère. Form a dozen gougères on the baking sheet, spacing them evenly. (If you have two buttered baking sheets, you can pipe out the remaining gougères on the second sheet while the first batch bakes, or pipe and bake both sheets at the same time.)

continued

Bake until the gougères just begin to show some color on top, 18 to 22 minutes. Take them out before they get too brown. Transfer to a wire rack and let them cool for at least 30 minutes before filling them.

To fill the gougères: Spoon one of the fillings—either the savory or chocolate version—into a pastry bag fitted with a tip or into a paper cone. Gently push the tip into a baked and cooled gougère from one side and squeeze in a little filling. Repeat with the remaining gougères. If you don't want to fool around with piping, slice a gougère halfway across from one side, taking care to not cut all the way through. Spoon in a little filling, and gently close the gougère.

Once you've filled the gougères, it's best to serve them within 6 hours. They can get slightly soggy if kept any longer. If you'd like to make them the day before, you can. Store them in an airtight container in a cool place and don't fill them until just before you plan to serve.

Dark Chocolate Filling

U.S.		METRIC
2½-oz	Chunk fine dark chocolate	70-g
8 oz	Mascarpone cheese	230 g
1 tsp	Ground espresso beans (not instant)	1 tsp
½ tsp	Sugar	½ tsp

With a microplane grater, finely grate the dark chocolate over the mascarpone. Stir in the ground espresso beans and sugar. Refrigerate in a tightly covered container for up to 48 hours until ready to fill the gougère.

Red Hawk Variation

If you want to add cheese to your gougères before they bake, use two wheels of Red Hawk instead of the Fromage Blanc Spreads. Follow the recipe and while piping each gougère onto the baking sheet stop when the gougère is three-quarters size. Add ½ tsp Red Hawk (or just drop a small chunk of Red Hawk onto the piped gougère) and then finish piping on top of the cheese. Bake as directed.

AGED CHEESES

PEOPLE ASK US OFTEN how we learned about cheese, and our answer is always the same: "We learned the cheeses one at a time."

We built our first cheese counter in Point Reyes in 1997 on a shoestring budget, selling just a dozen cheeses to start. The cheeses were tucked away at the end of our lunch counter. A single cabinet held geometric stacks of sturdy aged cheeses, and a small open refrigerator case held more delicate cheeses under shelves filled with cheese-friendly wines.

Our local cheeses were the featured stars of the counter. These included Matos St. George, Bellwether Farms Carmody and San Andreas, and Redwood Hill Farm Crottin.

We added new cheeses to our cases one at a time, and we made a conscious decision to add only "classic" imported cheeses. Our first cheese made outside of Northern California was a good, organic Parmesan that we found in the Rogers Collection, an importer of artisanal cheeses from Italy and Spain. After that we added Stilton, Montgomery's Cheddar, and Mrs. Kirkham's Lancashire that we bought from Neal's Yard Dairy in London.

Over time, we brought in cheeses from the limestone cellars of Jean d'Alos and a few excellent American cheeses from the East Coast and Wisconsin.

As we watch cheesemongers-in-training take on the Herculean task of quickly learning every cheese on the counter, we appreciate even more the fact that we got to educate ourselves very slowly, cheese by cheese.

UNDERSTANDING CHEESE CATEGORIES

These days we sell about a hundred types of cheese. When we hire a new cheesemonger, at first they focus on fresh cheeses before they're ready to sell the more complex aged cheeses.

Understanding how cheeses are categorized takes time because there really is no standard method for cataloging cheese. Cheesemakers in Italy use certain categories while French cheesemakers use other categories. This is a big hurdle to overcome when you're selling or buying cheese.

There's a reason for this: Most cheeses fall into more than one category. Look at Comté, Taleggio, and our own Red Hawk. All three are washed-rind cheeses, but they couldn't be more different from each other. The type of milk used, the place where the cheese was made, and the affinage—considering all these factors when buying cheese gives you a much better grasp than if you think in terms of "soft/bloomed rind" or "triple-crème."

A TOUR OF OUR CHEESE COUNTER

All three of our cheese shops—Point Reyes, San Francisco, and Washington, DC— display cheeses in the same presentation. A tour of our cheese shops might look something like this.

We start with the big, traditional, bandage-wrapped Cheddars and move on to cow milk cheeses with similar textures, including Matos St. George, Shelburne Farms Cheddar, and Beehive's Barely Buzzed.

From there we sample Gouda-style cheeses such as Wilde Weide from Holland and Pondhopper, a Gouda from Tumalo Farms in Oregon. Mountain-style cheeses come next, and we have a grand display of these washed-rind, savory cheeses, including Peggy's soft spot, Comté, as well as Gruyère, and Pleasant Ridge Reserve from Wisconsin.

Next stop on the tour is aged sheep milk cheeses. Get ready for cheese from the French Pyrénées, from the Tuscan region of Italy, Manchego from Spain, and some of our local favorites, including Baserri from Barinaga Ranch. Clustered in one corner of the shop are natural-rind aged goat cheeses, including Garrotxa from Spain and Pantaleo from Sardinia.

Grating cheeses, which are clustered at the far end of the counter, all have a story. Take Grana Padano, a cheese first made by Benedictine and Cistercian monks in Veneto's Padua Plain in the twelfth century. Or taste Dry Jack Special Reserve while you hear the story of the Vella family and their cheesemaking in California in the last century. Save for last the grand lady, Parmigiano-Reggiano, which has been made according to the same recipe for eight hundred years.

From here we move to the refrigerated cases. The soft aged blues and some of the younger aged cheeses such as Fontina are kept cool because their higher moisture content is not as stable at room temperature. Our cheese counters are beautiful and practical in part because of Debra Dickerson's expertise. For decades, Debra has taught hundreds of people how to taste, sell, and care for cheese. Selling these beautiful cheeses and adding more to our counter every year inspired us to create another cheese.

OUR SIXTH CHEESE: WAGON WHEEL

We made our first five cheeses for ten years before we felt it was time to develop an everyday aged cheese that could be used in cooking. We asked our friend Judy Rodgers, at Zuni Café, to help us develop a melting cheese that she might use on her famous pizza. Cowgirl Creamery cheesemakers Maureen Cunnie and Eric Patterson worked for months on this cheese. Eric was a very welcome addition to our team. Because Eric had managed his own farm earlier in his life, he had the ability to fix anything that broke down. Before Eric came along, Sue and Maureen sometimes felt that they were holding everything together with duct tape.

When Maureen and Eric came up with a cheese that we all loved, they got to present the winning cheese wheel to Judy. We named it Wagon Wheel in part because it was our first big wheel of cheese and because it's a delicious and versatile cheese, but not fancy. A more humble name seemed appropriate.

STIRRED-CURD CHEESE

Made with Straus organic milk and mesophilic and thermophilic cultures as well as traditional rennet, Wagon Wheel is a stirred-curd cheese. This means the curd is cooked and stirred, but not washed, which makes it a bit more acidic than the washed-curd cheeses. The curd is hooped into molds and pressed under heavy weights to expel more whey. It is then salted in a brine bath before going on the aging-room shelves. Many common cheeses are made using the stirred-curd method, including young block Cheddars and Monterey Jack. Although they may be salted and finished in their own unique style, stirred-curd cheeses share an excellent melting quality with our own Wagon Wheel.

WASHED-CURD CHEESE

In the last chapter, we talked about how we created Mt Tam and Red Hawk by starting with a Gouda recipe and shifting the method with each new version. Washing the curd means that part of the whey is drained off after the curd is cut and stirred, and replaced with warm water. Cheesemakers use this technique to coax the curd into releasing more whey, which reduces lactic acid flavors. Cheeses in this category include Gouda, Edam, Fontina, Colby, and Jarlsberg. They are distinguished by their dense, almost waxy textures, their sweet milky flavors, and excellent melting qualities. When allowed to age for longer than six months, amino acid crystals sometimes form, and after a year or so, these cheeses may become dry and flaky. When aged even longer, they may be classified as grating cheeses. More on grating cheeses in the next chapter, as soon as you learn just a little about Cheddaring.

CHEDDARING

Traditional Cheddars are unique in that after the curd is cut, cooked, and stirred, the whey is drained completely. The curd begins to knit together immediately, forming a firm mat at the bottom of the vat. This mat is then cut into big slabs, which are stacked on top of each other, usually four slabs high. Every ten minutes or so, the squares are restacked and turned until they reach the proper acidity, from half an hour to an hour. (This varies from one cheesemaker to another.) This backbreaking work pays off with a delicious cheese that is lower in moisture content than a stirred-curd cheese.

The next step in the Cheddaring process is milling. The curd slabs are put through a mill that sits across the vat. The mill works like a ricer, breaking the slabs of cheddar into bits that look a little like spaetzle. Next comes the salt, often stirred into the cheese with big tools that look almost like shovels. The point of this is to distribute the salt evenly throughout the curd. Next, the salted curd is hooped, which just means the milled curd is put into a cheese form before being pressed under weights. This cheese will end up being crumbly in texture and not very elastic. Traditional Cheddars are bandage-wrapped in strips of linen or cheese-cloth and then aged for two months to two years, and sometimes even longer. Natural molds are allowed to grow on the outside of the cheesecloth, and air exchange on the rind promotes deep, complex flavors in the cheese. Many English cheeses are made using this Cheddaring method, including Cheshire, Poacher, and Gloucester.

AGING AND CHEESE MITES

Aged cheeses with a craggy-looking rind are displaying the work of cheese mites. Mites are tiny organisms that feed on the rinds of certain cheeses, usually those with natural rinds such as Cheddar or Mimolette. The mites are so small that you can't see them without magnification, but you can easily notice the fine dusty brown residue they leave behind. As odd as it sounds, many cheesemakers delight in this evidence that cheese mites have arrived on the scene; a good number of cheese experts believe mites provide a limited amount of aeration that results in a better-tasting cheese. If you're a little unnerved by the idea of mites in your cheese, keep in mind that these are microscopic, much too small to be seen with the naked eye. Plus, they're found only in the rind, not in the paste of the cheese. One of the affineur's duties is to keep the mite population under control by routinely brushing the rinds and scrubbing the boards on which the cheese rests while aging.

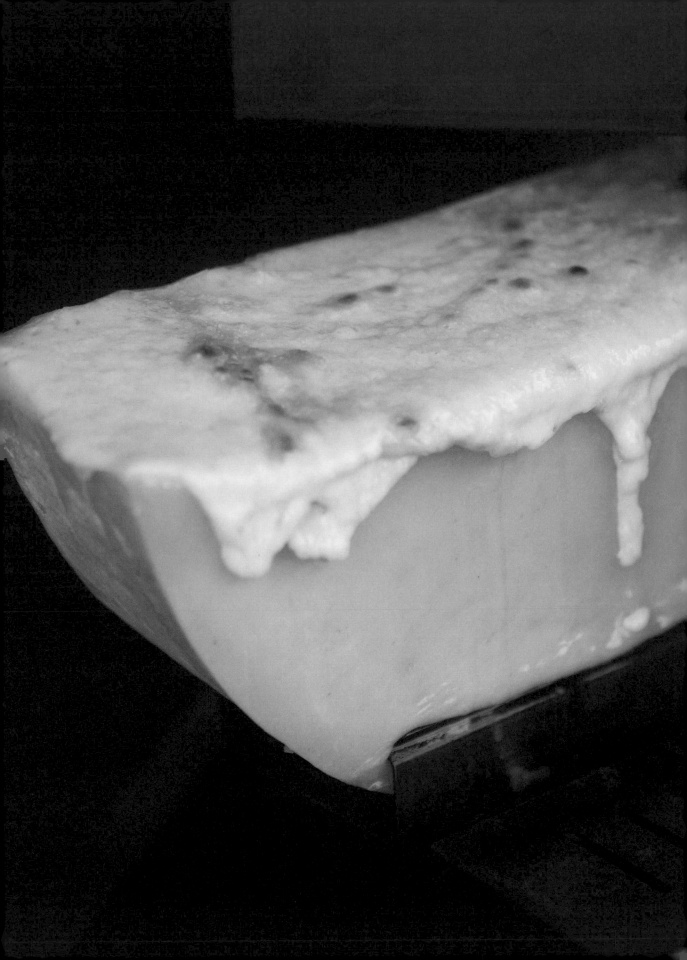

RACLETTE WITH BOILED POTATOES AND QUICK PICKLES

SERVES 6 TO 8

Traditional fare in the Raclette area of the Alps, this may be the simplest and most time-honored method of cooking cheese.

Raclette comes from the French word *racler,* which means "to scrape," and that's what you do: toast thick cheese slices and, when the cheese starts to bubble and brown, scrape off that good, melted, browned top layer onto boiled potatoes or crispy toast. Raclette isn't just a matter of melting the cheese; browning the top layer gives this dish its distinct and satisfying flavor. An indoor raclette grill, which is made to sit in the center of your dining table, or a *barbeclette* to use on an outdoor grill does this nicely, but if you don't own either tool, use a small skillet and brown the cheese right under your oven's broiler, while keeping a close watch (don't walk away while the raclette is in the oven or over the fire).

Crisp, acidic homemade pickles cut the buttery richness of the melted cheese. These pickles are quick and easy. Just heat the pickling solution; pour it over slices of squash, sliced onions, or halved baby carrots; and let the mixture sit for an hour. We like to make extra pickled vegetables; they keep in the refrigerator for weeks and are great in sandwiches. If you don't have time to pickle vegetables, serve raclette with cornichons.

Pickles

U.S.		METRIC
2	Medium zucchini, sliced into ½-in/1-cm rounds; or 1 red onion, peeled and sliced; or 2 handfuls of baby carrots, halved	2
½ cup	Water	120 ml
¾ cup	Red wine or Champagne vinegar	180 ml
1 tsp	Sea salt	1 tsp
1 tsp	Sugar	1 tsp
½ tsp	Pickling spice or red pepper flakes	½ tsp
½ tsp	Cloves	½ tsp
1½ lb	Yukon gold or new red potatoes	680 g
1 tbsp	Kosher salt	1 tbsp
6 to 8 oz	Raclette de Franche Comté cheese or Gruyère or Emmenthaler	170 to 225 g

continued

To make the pickles: Put the vegetables to be pickled in a large heatproof bowl. Combine the water, wine, sea salt, sugar, and pickling spice in a medium saucepan. Bring to a boil over medium-high heat. When the pickling solution is boiling, toss in the cloves and then pour the mixture over the vegetables. Let it sit for 1 hour. Pour into a glass container with all the liquid, cover, and refrigerate. The pickled vegetables will keep for up to 1 month in the fridge.

Start a fire in your outdoor grill (unless you have a tabletop electric raclette grill or you plan to broil the cheese in your oven).

While the vegetables are chilling in the refrigerator, put the potatoes in a medium pot and cover them with cold water. Bring the water to a boil over high heat. When the water boils, add the kosher salt, and decrease the heat to keep the water at a gentle simmer. Cook just until a potato is tender when pierced with a fork, about 10 minutes. Drain the potatoes, and set them aside while you prepare the cheese.

Sizes of raclette grills can vary, so slice the cheese to fit your raclette. If heating the cheese on an outdoor fire, make sure it has burned down to mostly grey coals with just a little glow of red.

To serve, spoon warm boiled potatoes and chilled pickled vegetables onto each plate. Scrape the melted cheese from the grilled and brown surface of the cheese that's been exposed to heat and eat this melting bit of cheese with a bite of the potatoes.

TOASTED FLATBREAD SANDWICHES, THREE WAYS

MAKES 2 SANDWICHES

For a fast meal or a quick snack, nothing beats a flatbread. You could make your own dough or buy some from a pizza shop and roll out and bake your own flatbread. We prefer to make these from rounds of store-bought naan bread or pita bread that we slice in half.

These sandwiches aren't open-faced like a pizza—they're more like a quesadilla. We like to cut the sandwiches in half, arrange on a plate, set out a pretty salad, and sit down at the table. But often when there's a group of friends and family hanging around, these get sliced up and devoured in the kitchen shortly after coming off the pan.

For our grilled cheese sandwiches (see pages 225–233) we use regular butter in the pan. For these flatbreads, we cook with clarified butter. Because grilled cheese takes longer to cook, we use a lower temperature and like the way the milk fats brown. For these flatbreads, which cook more quickly, the clarified butter helps prevent burning.

Cutting naan is an imperfect art. Use a serrated knife and don't worry if the bread tears. It will knit back together in the pan.

GOAT GOUDA WITH PARMESAN AND PARSLEY

We mix Gouda and Parmesan for this sandwich because the Gouda melts nicely and the Parm fills in with flavor and salt. Chop the fresh parsley into bigger pieces so you can really taste it.

U.S.		METRIC
8 oz	Gouda cheese, grated	230 g
4 oz	Parmesan cheese, grated	115 g
2 tbsp	Chopped fresh flat-leaf parsley	2 tbsp
1 tbsp	Clarified butter (page 242)	1 tbsp
2	Naan or pita breads, halved to make 4 rounds	2
½ tsp	Sherry vinegar	½ tsp

In a medium bowl, mix together the grated Gouda and Parmesan and the parsley.

Heat the butter in a skillet over medium heat. When it bubbles put in one bread round, cut-side up. Sprinkle on half of the cheese-parsley mixture. Top with the matching bread round, cut-side down. Let it heat for 2 to 3 minutes, and then turn the sandwich over using a spatula. Heat just until cheese is melted, another 2 to 3 minutes.

Transfer the flatbread to a plate, drizzle with the sherry vinegar, cut into quarters, and serve. Repeat with the remaining bread and cheese.

continued

LANCASHIRE WITH SWEET-HOT MUSTARD AND CHUTNEY

Almost any Cheddar will work for this flatbread, but we like the bright, lemony flavor of the Lancashire handcrafted by the Kirkham family; it's both creamy and crumbly when melted. Mixing the Lancashire with fromage blanc makes for an even creamier filling.

There's room to play with the mustard for this sandwich. If you have a sweet-hot Chinese-style mustard, mix it with a little maple syrup for a more mellow flavor. If you have only Dijon mustard, try mixing 2 tbsp mustard with 1 tbsp maple syrup and 1 tbsp honey.

U.S.		METRIC
4 oz	Grated Lancashire or Cheddar cheese	115 g
¼ cup	Fromage blanc	60 g
1 tbsp	Clarified butter (page 242)	1 tbsp
2	Naan or pita bread, halved to make 4 rounds	2
4 tbsp	Chutney (see page 89, or store-bought)	4 tbsp
2 tbsp	Mustard (see headnote)	2 tbsp

In a medium bowl, mix together the grated cheese and fromage blanc.

Heat the butter in a skillet over medium heat. When it bubbles, put in one flatbread round, cut-side up. Sprinkle on half of the cheese mixture. Let it heat for a minute or two while the cheese melts, then spoon on half the chutney. Spread some mustard on the cut-side of the matching flatbread round, and then place it on the sandwich in the pan, cut-side down onto the melted cheese. Let it heat for 2 to 3 minutes, and then turn the sandwich over using a spatula. Heat for another 2 to 3 minutes.

Transfer the flatbread to a plate, cut into quarters, and serve. Repeat with the remaining bread, cheese, chutney, and mustard.

continued

CHERYL'S WAGON WHEEL WITH HEIRLOOM TOMATOES AND SHALLOTS IN RED WINE VINEGAR

Cheryl Dobbins, who leads tours of our Point Reyes cheesemaking rooms, loves to add heirloom tomatoes to any grilled cheese. A mixture of red wine vinegar and balsamic vinegar adds just the right blend of acid and mellow undertones to the tomatoes in this filling. If you don't have Wagon Wheel, use a young Asiago or Fontina.

U.S.		METRIC
2 tbsp	Red wine vinegar	2 tbsp
1 tbsp	Balsamic vinegar	1 tbsp
1	Large shallot, minced	1
2	Medium tomatoes, cored and coarsely chopped	2
½ cup	Grated Wagon Wheel or Asiago cheese	115 g
2 tbsp	Grated Parmesan or Dry Jack cheese	2 tbsp
1 tbsp	Clarified butter (page 242)	1 tbsp
2	Naan or pita bread, halved to make 4 rounds	2

Mix the two vinegars in a medium bowl. Add the minced shallot and let it rest in the vinegar for 10 to 15 minutes. Add the chopped tomatoes to the bowl with the shallots and vinegar, stir, and let sit for a minute or two, and then pour through a fine-meshed strainer, reserving all the liquid. Set both the tomato-shallot mixture and the reserved liquid aside, in separate bowls.

In a medium bowl, mix together both the grated cheeses.

Heat the butter in a skillet over medium heat. When it bubbles, put in one bread round, cut-side up. Sprinkle on half of the cheese mixture. Let it melt for a minute or two and then spoon on half the tomato-shallot mixture. Top with the matching flatbread round, cut-side down. Let it heat for another minute, and then turn the sandwich over using a spatula. Cook for another 2 to 3 minutes.

Transfer the flatbread to a plate, cut into quarters, and serve with the reserved tomato juice–vinegar for dipping. Repeat with the remaining bread, cheese, and tomato-shallot mixture.

RED HAWK POTATO GRATIN

SERVES 6 TO 8

Because we love Red Hawk as a table cheese, we rarely cook with it, but this recipe is really good. This is the recipe our customers request most often.

U.S.		METRIC
2 tbsp	Unsalted butter	2 tbsp
2 tbsp	Extra-virgin olive oil	2 tbsp
1	Medium yellow onion, julienned	1
3	Garlic cloves, diced	3
1 cup	Heavy cream	240 ml
2 oz	Parmesan cheese, grated	45 g
2 lb	Yukon gold potatoes, peeled and thinly sliced	910 g
10 oz	Red Hawk cheese, cut into 16 wedges	280 g

Preheat the oven to 350°F/180°C/gas 4. Heat a cast-iron skillet or saucepan over medium-high heat. Add the butter and olive oil to the pan. When the butter has melted, add the onion and garlic and sauté until soft, about 5 minutes. Take the pan off the heat and add the cream and half of the Parmesan.

Transfer half of the onion-cream mixture to a glass 13-by-9-in/33-by-23-cm baking dish or casserole. Arrange half the thin potato slices in an overlapping, flat layer on top of the mixture, and then top with 8 of the Red Hawk wedges. Add the remaining potatoes, layering them evenly, the remaining half of the Red Hawk, and the remaining onion-cream mixture. Sprinkle with the remaining Parmesan.

Cover the dish with aluminum foil and bake for 45 minutes. Remove the foil and bake until the top is browned and bubbly, about 30 minutes. Let the casserole cool for 10 to 20 minutes. Serve while still warm. (This can be made a few days ahead and stored, tightly covered, in the fridge if you like. Reheat, covered, at 350°F/180°C/gas 4 for about 10 to 15 minutes.)

PANADE WITH GRUYÈRE AND ONION-GARLIC CONFIT

SERVES 4

A panade is a broth thickened with toasted cubes of levain or bâtard bread, creating a hearty, soulful soup. It's a lighter, fresher version of French onion soup, and can be served to vegetarians because it's made with a cheese broth instead of beef or veal stock. It's much faster to make than the old standard.

A mountain-style cheese such as Gruyère, Comté, or Pleasant Ridge Reserve works best here for two reasons: The cheese becomes elastic and holds its texture in the hot liquid, and the flavors of the soup—the yeasty bread and sweetness of the caramelized onions—are reminiscent of the flavors in the cheese.

The Onion-Garlic Confit gives this soup wonderful flavor, but if you like, you can make this recipe simpler by using chicken stock and quartered roasted onions, as shown in the photo.

U.S.		METRIC
4 cups	Bread cubes (about 1-in/2.5-cm cubes)	165 g
1 recipe	Onion-Garlic Confit (page 88)	1 recipe
6 cups	Parmesan Broth (page 236)	1.4 L
	Sea salt and freshly ground black pepper	
2 tbsp	Grated Gruyère or Comté cheese	2 tbsp
1 tsp	Sherry vinegar	1 tsp
1 tbsp	Fresh flat-leaf parsley (optional)	1 tbsp

Preheat the oven to 350°F/180°C/gas 4. Spread the bread cubes on a dry (not oiled) baking sheet. Toast the bread until dry throughout, but not browned, about 15 minutes. Set aside.

Combine the confit and broth in a large pan over medium heat. When the soup shows small bubbles, decrease the heat to low and let it simmer for at least 10 minutes. Taste and season with a pinch of salt and a few grinds of pepper (keeping in mind that the cheese contains salt, too).

For each serving, drop a handful of toasted bread cubes into an empty soup bowl. Sprinkle the grated cheese over the bread. Stir the sherry vinegar into the soup, and then ladle the soup over the bread and cheese in each bowl. Finish with a sprinkling of parsley, if you like. Serve right away.

MARY LOH'S CHEESE WAFERS

MAKES 55 TO 60 WAFERS

Mary Loh, Sue's mom, got this recipe from her mother, who was born in Macon, Georgia. In the Conley household, the holidays aren't complete without a few dozen batches of these, baked, packed in tins, and given to neighbors and cousins.

This dough is too stiff to mix by hand. You really need a stand mixer to get the dough right. Make the dough at least three hours before you plan to bake, so you can chill it. It's best to make the dough the night before. Top with pecan halves, if you wish.

U.S.		METRIC
2 cups	All-purpose flour	255 g
½ tsp	Sea salt	½ tsp
Pinch	Cayenne pepper	Pinch
½ lb	Unsalted butter, cut into chunks, at room temperature	225 g
1 lb	Sharp Cheddar cheese (very good quality), coarsely grated	455 g

Sift together the flour, salt, and cayenne and set aside.

In the bowl of a stand mixer fitted with the paddle attachment, cream the butter at medium speed until smooth. Decrease the speed to low and gradually add the cheese, in batches, until it's all been incorporated. Add the flour mixture ¼ cup/30 g at a time, waiting until each addition is thoroughly incorporated before adding more. The dough will be very stiff.

Lay flat a sheet of wax paper or plastic wrap. Spoon all the dough into a long cylinder, wrap it up tightly, and roll into a smooth, neat tube of dough that's about 1½ in/4 cm in diameter. Refrigerate for at least 3 hours or overnight.

When you're ready to bake, preheat the oven to 375°F/190°C/gas 5. Set out brown paper bags or parchment paper to rest the wafers on while they cool (Sue doesn't use wire racks to cool these).

Slice the dough into ¼-in/6-mm slices and place about 1 in/2.5 cm apart on an ungreased baking sheet. Bake until the wafers are golden brown on the top, and a deeper brown on the edges, 7 to 10 minutes.

With a spatula, transfer the wafers onto the paper to cool. They taste best when cooled for at least 30 minutes.

The wafers will keep for 2 weeks in a metal cookie tin, separated by layers of wax paper.

GRATING CHEESES

IN 2001, AMERICAN CHEESE EXPERT Jeff Roberts led a group of cheesemakers to the town of Bra, Italy, for the Slow Food Cheese Festival. The festival takes place every other year, but this was the first year that artisanal producers from the United States were invited to participate.

The town of Bra is where Carlo Petrini founded the grassroots organization Slow Food. This movement grew out of Carlo's alarm at the construction of a fast-food chain restaurant near the Spanish Steps in Rome, one of the most beautiful piazzas in the city. As the workers broke ground, Carlo wondered how this could happen in a country where meals are a relished event, where the tasks of growing and preparing food are honored and respected, and where people live for those beautiful moments spent together around the table.

Carlo felt that he had to do something to counteract the encroaching fast-food trend. Today, Slow Food is an international movement, with thousands of people working to preserve traditional foods, respect for the working landscape, and the farmers who sustain us all. The organization hosts a grand show of traditional Italian foods every other year called Salone del Gusto, and on the odd years moves the celebration to the tiny town of Bra. Here, the streets are closed to cars, allowing for a week-long, pedestrian-friendly cheese party. Cheesemaker booths wind through the streets with enthusiastic vendors offering tastes to cheese lovers who come from all over the world.

The Slow Food Cheese Festivals we've attended have given us a chance to expand our knowledge and make new connections. From dawn until midnight the chatter is all about cheese. Among the many tents and cheese booths, most represent the regions of Italy, but there is one grand tent lovingly referred to as Affineurs Alley, designed by Jason Hinds and David Lockwood of Neal's Yard Dairy. Inside the Affineurs Alley tent are groups of cheesemongers, affineurs, and producers representing France, Spain, England, Ireland, the Netherlands, Portugal, Germany, Switzerland, Austria, and the United States. There is even an Italian company or two inside the big tent.

In 2009, when a group of Americans were invited to exhibit at the show, one of our distributors, Atlanta Foods International, volunteered to sponsor six producers from the United States: Cypress Grove Chevre, Rogue Creamery, Vermont Creamery, Uplands Cheese Company, Jasper Hill Farm, and Cowgirl Creamery. The logistics were complex, and the event exhausting. But it reminded us of the days we spent in France working with the California winemakers at Vinexpo.

Here we were, after years of honing our craft, showing our cheese on the international stage. And to top it all off, the Italians went crazy for our Red Hawk.

Inside Affineurs Alley, the first booth belonged to Italian Parmigiano-Reggiano affineur Giorgio Cravero, representing a distinct group of Parmigiano producers. The Cravero family has been operating an aging facility for Parmigiano-Reggiano in downtown Bra for more than a century. The pristine, thick-walled structure maintains consistent cool temperatures, with perfect humidity for the 80-pound/ 36-kilogram rounds of cheese. The massive cheese wheels were lined up like soldiers on wood shelves stacked from floor to ceiling. We relished the opportunity to have a firsthand look at the process of aging the most loved of all grating cheeses.

Fine Grating Cheeses in California

Tom Vella had been working at the Sonoma Mission Creamery for almost a decade when a group of dairymen called on him. They wanted to know if he could make cheese, if they could provide a reliable source of milk. Tom felt he could, quit his day job, and before long the Vella Cheese Company was up and running.

When World War II hit, and all cheese imports came to a halt, Tom's cheese company ran at full capacity around the clock. The Vella Company's Dry Jack, pale and creamy with a delicate flavor, grew a devoted following and was often used in place of Parmigiano-Reggiano, which wasn't available.

Tom's son, Ignazio Vella, known to everybody in these parts as "Ig," continued to make Dry Jack and other handmade cheese in Sonoma until his death in 2011. The company is still in operation under the next generation, carrying on in Tom's and Ig's footsteps.

CHEESE FRICOS

MAKES 16 FRICOS

Traditional fricos are thin, crisp disks formed from small mounds of grated Parmesan, but you can make fricos from most hard-aged grating cheeses. Some folks like to add flour or spices to fricos, but we don't. We think the best fricos are made simply of cheese and used as a crispy finish to a salad or a bowl of polenta.

It's easiest to make fricos in your oven using parchment paper or a silicone baking sheet as the liner for a metal baking sheet.

U.S.		METRIC
4 oz	Parmesan cheese, grated (or any grating cheese)	115 g

Preheat the oven to 375°F/190°C/gas 5.

Line a baking sheet with parchment paper or a silicone baking sheet. Use a tablespoon to measure a spoonful of the grated cheese. With your fingers, shape the cheese into mounds, arranged about 4 in/10 cm apart.

Bake just until the fricos begin to color, turning golden brown, 2 to 4 minutes. It's easy to burn them, so as soon as you notice them darken and smell their fragrance, take them out of the oven. Let them cool on the baking sheet for 3 minutes and then use a metal spatula to transfer the fricos to a wire rack to cool completely.

If you like, you can make these up to 2 days ahead. Store them in an airtight container in a cool, dark spot with wax paper between them so they don't stick together.

WARM SPRING VEGETABLES WITH PECORINO AND ANCHOVIES

SERVES 6 TO 8

Some people believe that cheese tastes best with bread or potatoes, but we think a good cheese can enliven a vegetable dish like this one. A wide, thick piece of pecorino is best for this dish.

See tips for blanching asparagus on page 240, Cowgirl Kitchen Techniques.

We like the addition of anchovies, but if you're not a fan, you can leave them out and still have an excellent dish.

U.S.		METRIC
	Kosher salt	
3	Medium carrots	3
2	Medium zucchini	2
1	Leek, halved lengthwise and thoroughly cleaned	1
1 cup	Sugar snap peas	100 g
24	Thin asparagus spears	24
2 tsp	Extra-virgin olive oil	2 tsp
	Freshly ground black pepper	
2	Anchovy fillets, preferably salt-packed (see Preparing Anchovies, page 240; optional)	2
1	Head radicchio	1
½	Juicy lemon	½
2 oz	Aged Pecorino	55 g

Bring a large pot of water to a boil over medium-high heat, and add 2 tbsp salt. Have a large platter or baking sheet nearby for the blanched vegetables.

Meanwhile, cut the carrots and zucchini into sections that are 3 to 4 in/7.5 to 10 cm long. Slice each section into six or eight sticks. The carrot sticks and zucchini sticks should be about the same size.

Cut each leek half crosswise into half-moons about ½ in/12 mm wide. If the core of the leek is at all woody, discard it. The tender outer sections are best.

Decrease the heat to medium-low so the water stays at a gentle simmer. Blanch the vegetables one variety at a time, starting with the carrots. When the vegetables are no longer crunchy but are tender, slightly crisp, and still bright in color, take them out of the water with a slotted spoon, letting any water drain off. Put the vegetables out on a large platter or a baking sheet to cool, spreading them out so they don't continue to cook. Drizzle the olive oil over the warm vegetables and sprinkle with salt and pepper.

Put the cooled vegetables in a large bowl. Rinse the anchovies (if using) under cool running water. Try to slide your thumb under the spine, carefully separating the two fillets on either side. Chop the anchovies, add to the vegetables, and gently combine, tossing with your fingers until the anchovies are evenly distributed.

Spread the outer leaves of the radicchio on salad plates to form six to eight cups. Spoon an equal amount of the vegetables onto each radicchio cup, and top with a squeeze of lemon juice. Using a vegetable peeler, shave off five or six ribbons of cheese over the top of each cup before serving.

DRY JACK, ARTICHOKE, AND FENNEL SALAD

SERVES 6

This salad is unusual because every ingredient, including the artichoke, is raw. Whenever Peggy makes this beautiful salad, she thinks of her friend Catherine Brandel. Peggy and Catherine worked together at Chez Panisse. Catherine inspired both of us with her love of food and her approach to life. She was a noted anthropologist who was popular with her colleagues because she loved to cook for everyone at a dig. A true Renaissance woman, Catherine also illustrated science books and was an expert forager and avid gardener with an encyclopedic knowledge of ingredients.

Catherine began cooking downstairs at Chez Panisse as a fill-in, working for cooks on vacation, and then became a full-time chef in the Chez Panisse upstairs café. She and Peggy became good friends because they both had a similar style of cooking as well as the same subtle sense of humor. Together, Peggy and Catherine were awarded the Rising Chef award.

When Catherine died at the age of fifty-six, one of the things Peggy missed most about her was the hula. Catherine had spent part of her childhood in Hawaii, and danced the hula with the same precision and joy that she brought to her cooking. Even though Catherine is gone, our memories of her ending every party with a hula endure.

Lemon Dressing

U.S.		METRIC
6 tbsp	Extra-virgin olive oil	90 ml
2 tbsp	Freshly squeezed lemon juice	2 tbsp
1	Garlic clove, minced	1
½ tsp	Coarse sea salt	½ tsp
1	Shallot, minced	1
⅓ cup	Freshly squeezed lemon juice	75 ml
4	Medium artichokes	4
3	Large fennel bulbs, roots and feathery fronds trimmed (reserve fronds for garnish)	3
6	Celery stalks, sliced thinly on the diagonal	6
8	Large radishes, trimmed and julienned	8
12	Anchovy fillets	12
½ cup	Fresh flat-leaf parsley (leaves only)	30 g
	Sea salt and freshly ground black pepper	
3 oz	Dry Jack cheese, for shaving	85 g

continued

To make the dressing: In a medium bowl, whisk together the olive oil, 2 tbsp lemon juice, garlic, and salt. Set aside.

Pour the ⅓ cup/75 ml lemon juice into a large bowl. Work with a single artichoke at a time. Start by pulling off the small lower leaves. Snap off the larger leaves by holding the bottom of the leaf in place with your thumb while snapping the top of each leaf downward, leaving a thin bottom section of the leaf still in place on the choke. Using a paring knife, slice away the tough dark green outer leaves. Trim the base of the artichoke next to the stem and peel with a vegetable peeler. Use a teaspoon to scrape the fuzzy choke away from the heart. As soon as you've scraped away the choke, place the heart in the lemon juice. As you trim each artichoke, dunk it in the lemon juice and turn to coat. Toss occasionally to keep them coated with lemon juice, which keeps them from oxidizing and turning brown.

Using a mandoline or a very sharp chef's knife, slice each artichoke heart crosswise into thin sections. Put in the bowl and toss with lemon juice.

Remove any tough outer stalks from the fennel. Using a sharp knife or a mandoline, halve the bulbs from top to base. Slice these crosswise as thinly as you can into half-moons. Put in the bowl, toss with lemon juice to prevent oxidation, and set aside.

Whisk the dressing a few times. In a large bowl, toss the artichoke hearts, the fennel, celery, and radishes with a few spoonfuls of the dressing.

Arrange the vegetables on six plates. Sprinkle with sea salt and pepper and drizzle each salad with dressing. Use a vegetable peeler to shave wide ribbons of Dry Jack over each salad before serving.

CANTINA SALAMI SANDWICH WITH SAUTÉED GREENS AND AGED GOUDA

SERVES 4

Just right for picnics, this recipe proves that sandwiches made with grating cheeses don't have to be warm. Folks pick up this very popular sandwich in our Cowgirl Cantina in Point Reyes Station, and then head out to the coast knowing that lunch is in the bag.

American charcuterie has gotten more popular, so you can find good cured meat in every part of the country. Use any kind of cured meat that you like in this sandwich; poached or grilled chicken is delicious as well.

U.S.		METRIC
2 tbsp	Extra-virgin olive oil	2 tbsp
1	Yellow onion, diced	1
2	Garlic cloves, chopped	2
4 cups	Chopped Swiss chard	260 g
1 tbsp	Red wine vinegar	1 tbsp
½ tsp	Sea salt	½ tsp
	Freshly ground black pepper	
8 slices	Levain, sourdough, or olive bread	8 slices
2 oz	Fromage blanc	55 g
4-oz	Chunk aged Gouda	115-g
½ lb	Salami (or ham, mortadella, smoked turkey, chicken, or fish)	225 g

Heat the olive oil in a large pan or skillet over medium heat. Sauté the onion until translucent, about 8 minutes, and then add the garlic and cook just until it begins to show color, another 2 minutes. Add the chard, cooking and stirring occasionally until it's wilted down, 5 to 8 minutes. Take the pan off the heat. Transfer the chard to a plate to cool and sprinkle with the wine vinegar, salt, and pepper.

Spread one side of each bread slice with fromage blanc. Pile about ⅓ cup/75 g of the sautéed greens onto four of the bread slices. Using a vegetable peeler, shave off wide strips of Gouda over the greens on each sandwich. Add a good layer—as much as you like—of salami, ham, poultry, or fish. Wrap up the sandwiches and take on a picnic.

PARMESAN-CRUSTED CHICKEN PAILLARD

SERVES 3 TO 4

Paillards—scallopini in Italian—are very thin, boneless slices of any meat or poultry. You'll lightly pound the chicken (or the meat) so the slices are all an even thickness and cook uniformly.

Using this double-dip method of breading—first in an egg wash, then in grated Parmesan, back into the egg wash, and then in bread crumbs—results in the most beautiful golden-brown pieces of chicken, but don't stop there. You can use this same technique for veal or a pork or lamb loin. (We especially like thin slices of lamb crusted in grated Pecorino or Basque-style cheese.)

Finely grate the cheese and make sure your bread crumbs are about the same size.

We like to use clarified butter in the pan instead of oil, to accentuate the dairy flavors in the cheese crust. Having a nice amount of butter in the skillet ensures that the chicken cooks quickly all the way through before the cheese has time to melt.

U.S.		METRIC
1	Whole boneless, skinless chicken breast (about 1 lb/455 g), halved (or substitute veal, pork, or lamb loin)	1
2	Eggs	2
¼ cup	Half-and-half	60 ml
½ tsp	Fine sea salt	½ tsp
¼ tsp	Freshly ground black pepper	¼ tsp
1 cup	Finely grated Parmesan cheese	115 g
1 cup	Fresh bread crumbs (see page 241) or panko	110 g
	Clarified Butter (page 242)	

Slice the chicken into ½-in/12-mm slices, cutting diagonally to make the slices more even. A 1-lb/455-g whole chicken breast should give you about six larger slices (from the middle of the breast halves) and four small slices (from the edges). Lightly pound each slice just so they're all even and the same thickness.

Have two large plates or a large sheet of wax paper ready for the breaded chicken slices.

In a small, shallow bowl, mix the eggs, half-and-half, salt, and pepper with a fork. Put the cheese in another small, shallow bowl and the bread crumbs in a third bowl. (See Using the Wet-Hand/Dry-Hand Technique for Breading, page 242.)

Dip each chicken slice in the egg wash and then the cheese, back in the egg wash, and then in the bread crumbs. Set them on one of the plates, not touching each other.

Add the clarified butter to the skillet and heat over medium-high heat, making sure that there's at least ¼ in/12 mm of melted butter.

When the butter is hot, add enough chicken slices so the pan is filled but with some room between slices. These cook quickly; turn them over after 1 minute and see if they're browned. Cook until both sides are brown, 1 minute more, and then transfer to the second large plate. (Don't put these on paper towels, or the breading can come off.) Finish cooking the remaining slices.

These taste wonderful served warm, or cold the next day.

THREE-CHEESE LASAGNA
WITH MUSHROOMS AND SPINACH

SERVES 8 TO 10

We layer a lasagna the same way we top a pizza—with a light hand. Forget about over-stuffed layers and an overflowing casserole dish. You want to scatter just enough cheese and vegetables on the layers to flavor, but not overwhelm. If you use fresh pasta that's rolled very thin, you can even form eight or ten layers. With dried or thicker pasta sheets, you'll want fewer layers.

This delicate vegetarian lasagna plays up the cheese, complementing it with the flavors of mushrooms and spinach. Try experimenting with different types of mushrooms, but salt them sparingly as the Parmesan acts as salt in this dish.

You can use any fresh mushrooms you like. We use a combination of two-thirds crimini and one-third shiitake mushrooms for a good flavor without too much expense.

Don't worry about the size of your pan. Just make sure the pans you choose are deep enough to hold at least five layers.

U.S.		METRIC
2 tbsp	Dried porcini mushrooms	2 tbsp
3 cups	Milk (whole or low-fat)	720 ml
3 tbsp plus 1 tsp	Unsalted butter	3 tbsp plus 1 tsp
4 cups	Fresh spinach leaves	80 g
½ tsp	Sea salt	½ tsp
	Freshly ground black pepper	
1 tbsp	Extra-virgin olive oil	1 tbsp
1½ cups	Chopped yellow onion	225 g
4	Garlic cloves, chopped	4
6 cups	Sliced fresh mushrooms	450 g
2 tbsp	All-purpose flour	2 tbsp
1 lb	Fresh pasta sheets or dried lasagna noodles	455 g
8 oz	Gruyère or Comté cheese, grated	230 g
6 oz	Fromage blanc	170 g
1 oz	Parmesan cheese, grated	30 g

continued

Wrap the dried porcinis in cheesecloth tied with string. Heat the milk in a medium saucepan over medium-high heat until small bubbles form. Take off the heat and place the porcinis in the milk. Let it steep for 1 hour at room temperature.

Meanwhile, melt the 1 tsp butter in a large skillet over medium-high heat. Add the spinach, salt, and a few grinds of black pepper and decrease the heat to medium. Cook, tossing now and then, until the spinach has shrunk by half but is still green, about 3 minutes. Transfer the spinach to a bowl to cool. Wipe out the pan.

Heat the olive oil and 1 tbsp butter in the skillet over medium heat. When the butter is melted, add the onion and garlic to the pan. Sauté, stirring just until the onion softens; add the fresh mushrooms. Cook until the mushrooms begin to show some brown, about 10 minutes over medium heat. Take the pan off the heat and set it aside.

After 1 hour, squeeze as much milk as you can out of the porcinis into a bowl. Empty the mushrooms into another bowl and discard the cheesecloth.

Using the porcini-steeped milk, the remaining 2 tbsp butter, and the flour, make a béchamel, following the instructions in Mastering Béchamel, page 244.

Preheat the oven to 400°F/200°C/gas 6. Bring a large pot of water to a boil over medium-high heat for the pasta. Butter a lasagna pan or deep baking dish.

Cook the pasta and divide the mushrooms into three equal portions and the spinach into two equal portions, and have all the cheeses and béchamel ready for layering.

For the bottom layer, arrange the pasta starting at the pan's center and let the bottom half of each pasta sheet drape over the pan's sides. Sprinkle one-third of the mushrooms over the bottom pasta layer. Sprinkle lightly with one-third of the Gruyère. Add another pasta layer. Add béchamel sauce, smoothing it over the pasta. Arrange half the spinach on the pasta and top with half the fromage blanc, dropping small spoonfuls on top of the spinach. Add another neat layer of pasta. Repeat with another mushroom and Gruyère layer, more pasta, and another béchamel, spinach, and fromage blanc layer. After the final mushroom layer, fold over the pasta edges that have hung over the pan sides all this time. Give the top a final light layer of béchamel, smoothing it evenly over the pasta, sprinkle with Parmesan, and cover the top with aluminum foil.

Bake for 20 minutes, then remove the foil and decrease the oven temperature to 350°F/180°C/gas 4. Cook until the cheese on top is bubbly and starting to brown, another 15 to 20 minutes. Take the lasagna out of the oven and let it cool for at least 15 minutes before serving.

BLUE CHEESES

IN A SURPRISINGLY SHORT TIME IN THE AGING ROOM, blue cheese can develop a wide range of flavors: Caramel, earthy notes, dark chocolate, a lemony tang, and roast beef are just some of the flavors that can emerge. Most blues spend less than two months in the caves, and yet the flavors in blues are among the most dynamic found in cheeses.

Most blue cheeses are made with fresh, lightly pressed curd, similar to fromage blanc curd. The loosely knit, high-moisture medium allows tiny open spaces in the paste of the cheese in which blue mold can grow. The blue mold, which is added to the milk along with rennet and cultures, develops only on surfaces where oxygen is introduced. Long, thin needles are used to pierce the cheese after it has been formed into a wheel and salted. Blue veins form along the paths of the needle piercings as the cheese ages and also on rinds that are exposed to oxygen.

Point Reyes has a great blue cheese story. We remember when the Giacomini family first met Jeffa Gill, a cheesemaker visiting from Ireland.

Bob and Dean Giacomini purchased a farm near Point Reyes in 1959. Through the ups and downs of the commodity milk market, they were able to run a profitable Holstein dairy there for decades, but they were looking into cheesemaking as a way to secure a future for the next generation.

At this same time, many dairy farmers in West Marin were realizing that they had to come up with value-added farm products if they wanted to survive and stay in business. Enter Ellie Rilla, farm advisor with the University of California Cooperative Extension, who has encouraged West Marin dairy farmers in many ways over the years. Ellie worked with the California Milk Advisory Board to bring in Jeffa Gill to teach a cheesemaking class in our barn in 1998.

County Cork is considered the center of Ireland's artisan cheese movement. For us, it was interesting to discover that the Irish artisan cheesemakers were only a few years ahead of American cheesemakers. Jeffa was a kindred spirit. Over the years we would find food entrepreneurs like Jeffa in County Cork in Ireland, Covent Garden in London, and Berkeley.

Bob brought his daughters—Lynn, Diana, Jill, and Karen—down to our barn for Jeffa's class. Jeffa inspired all of us that day with tales of making small batches of cheese on the farm using milk from her own cows. Her story convinced many of the ranchers in the room that they could start small and slowly build production over time. We could see on the Giacominis' faces when they realized that small-production cheesemaking on their ranch was entirely within reach.

Soon after that class, the Giacominis began moving ahead with their plan of making a really good American blue cheese right on the farm. Their cheese is called Point Reyes Original Blue, and it's a great one.

Stilton

One of our favorite blues, Stilton is often referred to as the "King of English cheeses." Made in the Midlands region of Great Britain since the 1700s, Stilton is aged in caves that, after centuries, swarm with blue molds along with many other wild molds and bacteria native to the region. Unlike Danish blue cheeses, in which the rind is wrapped and protected from stray molds, with Stilton, molds are encouraged to grow freely on the rind after the cheese has been pierced. The result is an incredibly luscious texture on the cheese within.

Roquefort

After Comté, Roquefort is France's most popular cheese. Legend has it that Pliny the Elder sang its praises in A.D. 79. Even then it was heralded for its rich flavor. Creamy, salty, and intense, Roquefort is aged for ninety days in natural caves in AOC-designated regions. The blue veins in this cheese are more greenish-blue, a color the French refer to as *persille* (parsley), and the flavor is rich and piquant.

Many centuries-old Roquefort caves contain so much blue mold growing on the walls that there's no need for cheesemakers to inoculate.

Fourme d'Ambert

Considered one of the oldest cheeses in France, this cheese dates back to the Roman conquests and is now protected by AOC regulations. Named for its shape, Fourme d'Ambert is a cylinder with a natural rind that resembles rough stone. Made with pasteurized cow milk from the Auvergne region, this pale, cream-colored, velvet-soft cheese is veined with blueing. This savory cheese has dark notes of bittersweet chocolate, tobacco, and damp earth.

Gorgonzola: Two Types—Piccante and Dolce

During a year or more of aging, Gorgonzola piccante is washed repeatedly with brine. The cheese develops a powerful aroma and sticky rind, with an ivory paste shot through with marks that tend toward blue. Spicy and earthy, piccante is the sharper and more aggressive of the two gorgonzolas.

Gorgonzola dolce, a blue cow milk cheese, is rich with fresh notes of grass. It's moister, softer, and creamier than its older sister, Gorgonzola piccante, because dolce is aged for only three months, while piccante is aged for a year or more. Gorgonzola dolce, like piccante, is washed repeatedly in brine. This cheese develops an aromatic buttery yellow paste with greenish striations.

FRIED SQUASH BLOSSOMS WITH FILBERTS AND BAYLEY HAZEN BLUE

SERVES 4

We really like the contrast of these squash blossoms: lightly crisp outside, warm and melting inside; comfort food and yet beautiful enough for a dinner party. The easiest squash blossoms to fill are the ones you pick yourself from your garden because just-picked blossoms are more pliable. If you buy them, make sure the petal part of the flower looks fresh and not limp. A pastry bag makes filling the blossoms easier, but you can use a spoon, too. Leave the trailing end at the tip of the bloom so the cheese stays inside. Because these are rich, one blossom per person is plenty.

Brothers Andy and Mateo Kehler of Jasper Hill Farm in Vermont make Bayley Hazen Blue, which is named after an old military road that was named after two Revolutionary War heroes. You can stuff a squash blossom with any blue cheese, but we like the drier, more crumbly blues for this recipe. Lemon zest is especially good because it mellows out the stronger flavors when cooking with blues.

Filling

U.S.		METRIC
2 tbsp	Fromage blanc	2 tbsp
2 tbsp	Blue cheese (preferably a dry, crumbly blue such as Bayley Hazen)	2 tbsp
2 tsp	Finely chopped hazelnuts	2 tsp
	Freshly ground black pepper	
1½ tsp	Freshly grated lemon zest	1½ tsp
1 tsp	Freshly squeezed lemon juice, plus more if needed	1 tsp
4	Fresh squash blossoms	4
1	Egg yolk	1
1 tbsp	Whole milk	1 tbsp
⅔ cup	Coarsely ground cornmeal, plus more if needed	80 g
	Sea salt	
	Peanut oil, for frying	

continued

U.S.		METRIC
2 tbsp	Sherry vinegar	2 tbsp
2 tbsp	Balsamic vinegar	2 tbsp
3 tbsp	High-quality olive oil	3 tbsp
2 cups	Mizuna or mixed salad greens	40 g
4 slices	Toasted dark levain bread, for accompaniment	4 slices

To make the filling: In a bowl, blend both cheeses, the nuts, ¼ tsp black pepper, and lemon zest. Squeeze on the lemon juice, taste, and add more juice if you like. Spoon the mixture into a pastry bag, if using.

Use your fingers to gently open the blossoms from the tip, taking care not to tear the petals. With the pastry bag, or using a spoon, fill each blossom with the cheese mixture. Don't overstuff them; they shouldn't expand like a balloon. Just put in enough cheese so they are filled from base to tip. When each blossom is filled to the top, gently roll the blossom on a work surface to evenly distribute the cheese inside.

In a small bowl, whisk together the egg yolk and milk. Set aside. Pour the cornmeal onto a small plate and add a pinch of salt, mixing with a fork.

Dredge a stuffed squash blossom in the egg wash and then in the cornmeal. (See Using the Wet-Hand/Dry-Hand Method of Breading, page 242.) Repeat with the remaining squash blossoms, adding more cornmeal to the plate if needed.

Pour enough peanut oil into a 10-in/25-cm or larger skillet or saucepan so that you have about ½ in/12 mm of oil. Heat the oil over medium-low heat until the oil registers 220°F/110°C on a deep-fat thermometer. (You don't want too high a flame, or the cheese will weep and melt too quickly.) If you don't have a thermometer, test if the oil is ready by tossing a few cornmeal grains into the pan. If the oil sizzles, it's hot enough.

These cook quickly. Cook until the cornmeal becomes lightly crisp and golden, for no more than 30 seconds. Transfer to a plate to cool just for a few minutes while you dress the salad.

In a small bowl, make a dressing by whisking together both vinegars, the olive oil, and ½ tsp salt. Season with pepper. Put the mizuna in a medium bowl. Lightly dress the greens and mound equal amounts on four plates. Add a squash blossom and a slice of levain toast to each plate, and serve immediately.

SWEET SMOKEY BLUE AND BACON SOUFFLÉ

SERVES 8

This soufflé uses the same method as the Ricotta-Asparagus Soufflé (page 114) but the flavor couldn't be more different. Rogue Creamery's Smokey Blue is an ideal cheese to use in this recipe because the smoky flavor works so well with the bacon.

U.S.		METRIC
1 cup	Whole milk or half-and-half	240 ml
4	Fresh eggs, separated	4
2 tbsp	Unsalted butter	2 tbsp
2 tbsp	All-purpose flour	2 tbsp
1 cup	Blue cheese, crumbled	130 g
⅛ tsp	Freshly ground black pepper	⅛ tsp
Pinch	Cayenne pepper	Pinch
4	Bacon strips, cooked crisp and chopped into bits	4

Preheat the oven to 450°F/230°C/gas 8. Butter a 10-in/25-cm baking dish and set aside.

Whisk together the milk and egg yolks (the whites will be used in the soufflé) in a medium bowl and set aside. Add the butter to a medium saucepan over medium heat. (Don't use a nonstick or coated pan.) When it's sizzling, add the flour and whisk constantly until the mixture shows some color. Don't let it turn brown. Keep whisking while you slowly pour in the milk–egg yolk mixture. If the butter and flour seize up, just keep whisking. Let the mixture cook over medium heat— keep whisking—until it thickens slightly, about 1 minute. When the sauce has a velvety texture, stir in ½ cup/65 g of the blue cheese, the black pepper, and cayenne. Set the pan aside to cool.

Whisk the egg whites until they hold a gentle peak. Don't overbeat, or you'll break the proteins and the whites won't expand as much during cooking.

Stir the bacon bits into the sauce. Fold in about half of the egg whites. Very delicately fold in the last of the egg whites and the remaining blue cheese and pour the mixture into the prepared pan.

Bake the soufflé for 7 minutes and then decrease the heat to 400°F/200°C/gas 6. Bake until the soufflé is lightly browned on top and a skewer inserted in the center comes out clean, 10 to 12 minutes. Serve right away.

BAKED ENDIVE AND PEARS IN BLUE CREAM SAUCE

SERVES 4 TO 6

This is one of our favorite ways to cook with blue cheese. Layer the sweet slices of juicy pear between the endive and then pour a velvety blue cheese sauce over the top before baking. It's a wonderful dish if you're having guests for dinner but it's also easy enough to make for yourself on a weeknight, and it tastes even better as leftovers the next day.

Comice and Anjou pears work beautifully because they hold together when heated.

Blue Cream Sauce

U.S.		METRIC
½ cup	Heavy cream	120 ml
3 oz	Creamy blue cheese (such as Point Reyes Original Blue)	85 g
2 tbsp	Chopped fresh chives	2 tbsp
	Freshly ground black pepper	
6	Endive, halved from stem to tip	6
2	Large pears, peeled, cored, halved, and cut into thin slices or wedges	2

To make the sauce: Pour the cream into a saucepan set over medium heat. With your fingers, break apart the blue cheese into the cream. Heat, stirring, just until hot (it's okay if the chunks of blue don't entirely smooth out). Take the pan off the heat, stir in 1 tbsp of the chopped chives and season with pepper. Set aside.

Preheat the oven to 425°F/220°C/gas 7. Butter a baking dish. Any medium baking dish will work.

In the baking dish, arrange the endive, cut-side up, alternating stem end and tip. Arrange the pears between each endive half. If you have more endive than can fit in one layer, top with the remaining endive halves, cut-side down. Pour on the cream sauce. The endive should not be submerged. Cover the baking dish with aluminum foil.

Bake for 15 minutes and then remove the foil. Continue cooking until the cream sauce has reduced slightly and the tops of the endive are browned, another 20 to 25 minutes.

Let the dish cool for at least 10 to 15 minutes, and then spoon up and enjoy while still warm. This is also very good cold the next day.

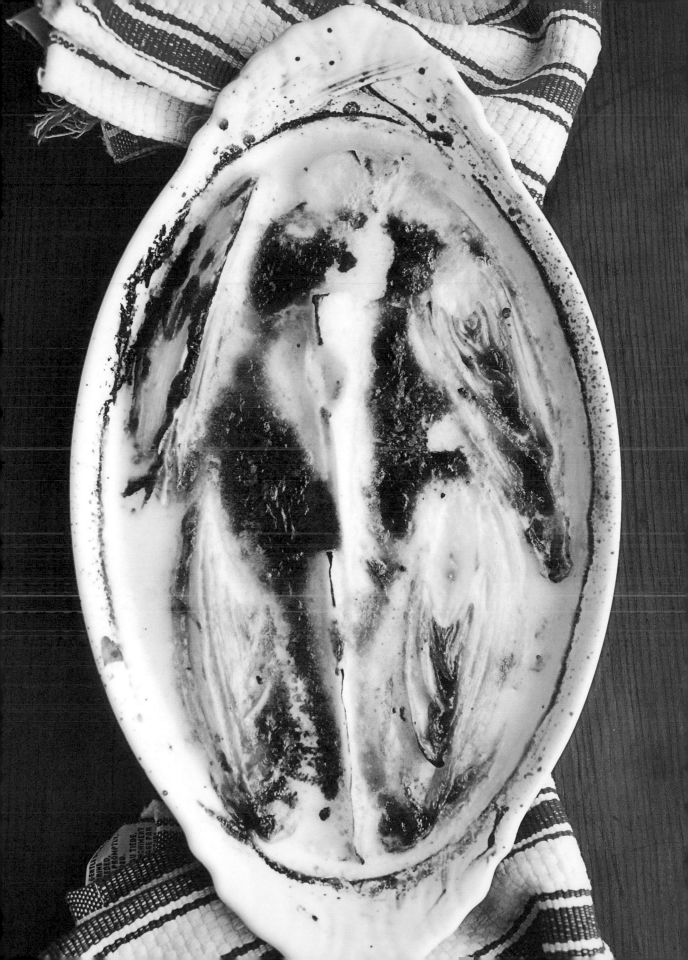

BLUE CHEESE FRITTATA WITH YAMS, PANCETTA, AND CHIVES

SERVES 4

Called a *frittata* in Italy, this egg-potato-cheese omelet is called a *tortilla* in Spain—a bit confusing to those of us in the States who think of tortillas as flat rounds of masa.

No matter what it's called, this combination works very well with the unexpected addition of blue cheese, which sparks up the flavor. This is a good technique to have in your repertoire because as long as you have yams (or potatoes), eggs, and cheese in the house, you have a simple, easy dinner ready in a few minutes. Take the eggs, cheese, and half-and-half out of the fridge about 15 minutes before you make this. The mixture rises better in the oven if the ingredients are about room temperature when you begin.

U.S.		METRIC
½ tsp	Kosher salt	½ tsp
1	Medium yam, peeled and cut into 1-in/2.5-cm cubes	1
¼ cup	Chopped pancetta, cut into ½-in/12-mm) pieces	55 g
6	Eggs	6
¼ cup	Half-and-half	60 ml
¼ tsp	Cayenne pepper	¼ tsp
1½ tsp	Chopped fresh flat-leaf parsley	1½ tsp
1 tsp	Chopped fresh chives	1 tsp
¼ cup	Creamy blue cheese	35g

Have a baking sheet or heat-proof platter nearby for the yam.

Add the salt to a small saucepan half-full of water and bring to a boil over medium-high heat. Add the yam cubes, decrease the heat to medium, and cook until the yam is tender, about 12 minutes. With a slotted spoon, take the yam out of the water and spread on a baking sheet to cool, so the cubes lose some of their moisture.

Preheat the oven to 400°F/200°C/gas 6. In an 8- or 9-in/20- or 23-cm skillet or saucepan (nonstick if you like), sauté the pancetta over medium heat until crispy, about 10 minutes. Take the pan off the heat but leave the pancetta in the pan.

Mix the eggs with the half-and-half, cayenne, 1 tsp of the parsley, and the chives. Pour the herbed eggs into the pan on top of the pancetta. Scatter on a mounded ½ cup/120 g of the yam; don't use more than you need. (Refrigerate any leftover yam for another use.) Crumble the blue cheese on top of the yam, and put the pan in the oven.

Bake the frittata until it is puffed and brown in places on the top, about 20 minutes. Take it out of the oven and let it sit in the pan for 1 to 2 minutes, and then flip the pan over onto a plate. Sprinkle the remaining ½ tsp parsley on top and serve.

NANCY KNICKERBOCKER'S CRUMBLED
BLUE CHEESE VINAIGRETTE

MAKES ABOUT ¾ CUP/180 ML

From the beginning, Peggy Knickerbocker has always lent us a helping hand along with sage advice. Peggy helped us find our first San Francisco shop location and sent all her friends to shop at our store, and she's helped us with everything from decorating to cooking tips.

This recipe is a case in point. When we asked her if we could include her excellent blue cheese vinaigrette in our cookbook, not only did she graciously send the recipe (and attribute it to her mother, Nancy), but she included the next recipe for Betty Barham's Creamy Blue Cheese Dressing as well. That's just like Peggy—to give us what we need and then a little extra gift as well.

Peggy visits our shop in the Ferry Building in San Francisco every single Saturday. She always explores the blue cheese selection first, and never goes home empty-handed.

U.S.		METRIC
1	Large shallot, minced	1
Pinch	Fine sea salt	Pinch
Pinch	Freshly ground black pepper	Pinch
1 tbsp	Sherry vinegar	1 tbsp
½ tsp	Good balsamic vinegar	½ tsp
⅓ cup	Extra-virgin olive oil	75 ml
3 oz	Roquefort-style blue cheese	85 g

In a medium bowl, combine the shallot, salt, pepper, and both vinegars. While whisking, slowly pour in the olive oil. With your fingers, crumble the blue cheese over the bowl. Turn it with a spoon so the crumbles are coated with the vinaigrette.

Serving suggestions: Spoon the vinaigrette over endive leaves, romaine leaves, or Little Gem lettuces. Finish with thin slices of crisp pear and a handful of roasted pecans or walnuts, if you like.

BETTY BARHAM'S CREAMY BLUE CHEESE DRESSING

MAKES ABOUT 2 CUPS/475 ML

This is a dressing from the 1950s that's now back in vogue (or maybe it never went out of style). Our friend Peggy Knickerbocker got this recipe from her friend, winemaker Barbara Barham Mendelsohn. Barbara would joke that her mother, Betty Barham, made only three recipes: double-cut lamb chops, a caviar pie of lumpfish caviar or salmon eggs, and this perfectly balanced dressing with big chunks of blue in a creamy, tangy base. If you make only three recipes, this would be a good one to know.

For the best flavor, make this dressing at least 12 hours in advance. 24 hours ahead is even better.

U.S.		METRIC
5 oz	Buttermilk blue cheese	140 g
1	Large shallot	1
	Fine sea salt	
¾ cup	Sour cream	180 ml
¼ cup	Milk or half-and-half, plus more if needed	60 ml
⅓ cup	Mayonnaise	75 ml
	Freshly ground black pepper	

In a large bowl, crumble the blue cheese with your fingers. Grate the shallot over the cheese, and then add ¼ tsp salt, the sour cream, milk, and mayonnaise. Season with pepper. Stir it all together, taste, and add more salt and pepper if you like.

Cover and refrigerate for 12 to 24 hours before serving. If the dressing is too thick, add more milk, a spoonful at time, until it's the right consistency. This will keep in your refrigerator for up to 1 week.

Serving suggestions: Betty would pour her dressing over iceberg lettuce wedges (another dish that's back in fashion), but you can also spoon this on romaine hearts. Top with crisp bacon crumbles and a good fresh grinding of black pepper.

BLUE BUTTER ON GRILLED RIB-EYE

SERVES 4

Sizzling steaks hot off the grill (or pan-seared on your stove) taste better when topped with a rich, creamy blue cheese compound butter. Rib-eye or porterhouse cuts of beef work well here; choose thick steaks and take them out of the refrigerator about 30 minutes before you plan to cook them.

If you can find it, add a dash of Pickapeppa sauce to the blue butter. If you can't find it, Worcestershire is a good substitution.

If you have leftover blue cheese, this compound butter is a great way to use it because you can freeze it for up to 3 months.

Blue Butter

U.S.		METRIC
¼ cup	Blue cheese (preferably Point Reyes Original Blue)	35 g
2 tbsp	Unsalted butter, at room temperature	2 tbsp
2 dashes	Pickapeppa or Worcestershire sauce	2 dashes
1 tbsp	Finely chopped fresh chives	1 tbsp
2	Bone-in rib-eye steaks, each about 1 lb/455 g and 1½ in/4 cm thick	2
2 tbsp	Extra-virgin olive oil	2 tbsp
2 tbsp	Sea salt	2 tbsp
	Freshly ground black pepper	

To make the blue butter: With a fork, mash together the cheese and butter with the Pickapeppa in a medium bowl. When the cheese is evenly distributed, stir in the chives. Chill the compound butter if using the same day or roll into a log, wrap tightly in plastic wrap, and freeze for up to 3 months (see Making and Storing Compound Butter, page 242).

Lightly coat each side of the steaks with olive oil. Sprinkle salt and pepper on each side and lightly press into the meat with your fingers. Get a cast-iron skillet (two, if you have them) smoking hot, either at your grill or on your stove. Place a steak on the hot pan and lower the lid of your grill, if grilling. Let them cook for 6 to 10 minutes, depending on whether you'd prefer rare or medium-well beef. Turn the steaks over and cook for another 6 to 10 minutes.

Spoon 3 tbsp of the butter onto each of the steaks, while hot, and serve right away.

BLUE AND CHEDDAR WAFERS WITH WALNUTS

MAKES 55 TO 60 WAFERS

These crisp rounds are based on Mary Loh's Cheese Wafers (page 164) but taste completely different. Blue cheese gives them a depth and sharpness that may be an acquired taste. Folks who love these really love them. If you're a fan of blue cheese, this is a wafer you'll want to try.

This dough is incredibly stiff—too stiff to mix by hand. You need a stand mixer to get the dough right. Make the dough at least three hours before you plan to bake, and overnight is best so the dough has time to chill.

U.S.		METRIC
½ lb	Sharp Cheddar cheese	225 g
6 oz	Stilton-style blue cheese	170 g
2 cups	All-purpose flour	255 g
½ tsp	Freshly ground black pepper	½ tsp
½ lb	Unsalted butter, cut into chunks, at room temperature	225 g
¼ lb	Walnut halves	130 g

Coarsely grate the two cheeses together into a large bowl and set aside. Sift together the flour and black pepper into another large bowl and set aside.

In the bowl of a stand mixer fitted with the paddle attachment, cream the butter at medium speed until smooth. Decrease the speed to low and add the cheese, in batches, until it's all been incorporated. Add the flour mixture ¼ cup/30 g at a time. The dough will be very stiff.

Lay flat a sheet of wax paper or plastic wrap on a work surface. Spoon all the dough into a long cylinder, wrap it up tightly, and roll it into a neat tube of dough that's about 1½ in/4 cm in diameter. Refrigerate for at least 3 hours or overnight.

When you're ready to bake, preheat the oven to 375°F/190°C/gas 5. Set out brown paper bags or parchment paper to rest the wafers on while they cool (Sue doesn't use wire racks to cool these).

Slice the dough into ¼-in/6-mm slices, and place about 1 in/2.5 cm apart on an ungreased baking sheet. Top each dough slice with a walnut half. Bake until the wafers are golden brown on the top, and a deeper brown on the edges, 7 to 10 minutes.

With a spatula, transfer the wafers onto the paper to cool. They taste best when cooled for at least 30 minutes.

The wafers will keep for two weeks in a metal cookie tin, separated by layers of wax paper. If you put them in an airtight plastic container, they won't keep as long; they'll soften too much.

THE END BITS

WHO KNEW THAT CARING FOR WHEELS OF MOLDY CHEESE in a dark, cool cave could be a satisfying life-long occupation? We learned about this underground world in 1995 when Jason Hinds and David Lockwood of Neal's Yard Dairy invited us to stop in at their Covent Garden shop in London.

From the street, you'd never guess what went on behind the classic London storefront. The narrow retail area is designed for one-on-one service. There is a long counter down one side where cheesemongers greet customers and sell their cheeses. The counter is piled with English classics including Stilton, linen-wrapped Cheddar, Caerphilly, Lancashire, and Cheshire. The cheeses are stacked in towers so high that they form small turrets. We arrived before the store opened for the day, and the staff was in the process of building dramatic cheese towers with a solid whole wheel as the base, then a half wheel, then a quarter wheel, topped by a delicate dome of several smaller wedges.

On the other side of the shop, narrow shelves displayed all kinds of locally made jams, breads, and a few special imported European goods, leaving just enough space in the middle for two people to pass from one end of the room to the other. In between serving retail customers, the cheesemongers prepared whole-sale orders for retailers and restaurant chefs. Cheeses were cut to the specification of the chef and delivered to the account that very same day.

During this visit, we spent some time behind the counter, learning how to properly care for cheese. Before each slice, the cut surface of the cheese is scraped with a knife: This eliminates the top layer, which can oxidize (and lose flavor) when exposed to air. Before any decision is made, the customer is offered tastes of the cheesemonger's recommendations as well as any cheese they'd like to try. The cheese is then cut to the customer's specifications. The rest of the cheese is carefully placed back in the display.

After we watched the retail operation in action, we were led downstairs into three small rooms, where a young and exuberant crew practiced the art of cheese affinage. David helped us suit up in white coats, sporty white caps with short brims, and Wellies, and off we went. The first room was lined with thick wooden shelving filled with cheeses showing moldy and mottled rinds. The next room had similar shelves, loaded with the same cheeses that were in the first room, only younger. In order to increase the humidity in this room, a homemade fountain had been set up using plastic tubing, aquarium pumps, and 5-gallon/19-litre tubs. The contraption forced water up from a bucket on the floor, through a plastic tube, to the top tub in a stack of tubs. The water cascaded slowly down from tub to tub, bringing up the moisture level in the space.

The third room, no bigger than a standard closet, held delicate soft-ripened cheeses and washed-rind cheeses. Each batch was labeled with a turning schedule written on a tag that hung from each rack. Each stack of racks was divided by a tidy white shower curtain serving as makeshift walls designed to control air flow and humidity.

While each room was pristinely clean, there was a very appealing rigged-up quality to the setup; we got the sense that Neal's Yard wanted to make each environment perfectly right for the cheese but imagination and creativity took over where the budget was tight. The lower level may have been built in an economy-driven way, but each room had its own personality that matched the cheeses stored there. At first glance the lower level seemed like a maze, but as we were shown each room, the order of the entire level became clear.

Every time we go to Neal's Yard, we learn something new. Perfectionists as well as innovators, the Neal's Yard folks will go to incredible lengths to enhance the quality of their cheese. They redo their aging rooms often and improve them with every incarnation. We knew that each cheese required a specific temperature and humidity during aging, but the folks at Neal's Yard showed us how they created environments specifically attuned to the needs of each cheese. Their cellars were pristine, meticulously maintained from the gleaming red-tiled floor with the drain at the center to the racks weighted down with lovely cheeses.

Perhaps one of the most memorable parts of this visit was meeting Beth Carlson, the keeper of one of the aging rooms. Beth's job was to care for each cheese and to know when the cheeses needed to be brushed, turned, and washed. She nodded hello as we walked in but continued doing what she'd been doing—brushing and wiping cheeses as she sang to them. Beth didn't hold back. If anything, she seemed to appreciate the audience and amplified the volume. She made up songs about every cheese. We didn't stop to write down the lyrics but remember them being along the lines of "Oh, you must have been a beautiful baby Stilton, but, baby, look at you now. Time for a good brushing now, baby."

Beth inspired us. She spent most working hours in a small, dimly lit, moist underground room, but the joy she expressed in her craft and her affection for her cheeses were obvious. Her songs lifted our spirits. She recognized that each cheese has a personality and requires individual care. We still think about Beth years later, and the thought of her always brings a smile. Although we don't sing to our cheeses (when anyone else is within hearing distance), we believe each and every cheese deserves its own song of tribute.

A few principles that we learned at Neal's Yard Dairy will help you care for the cheeses you buy. Cheese is an ever-changing food. Aged cheeses age from the inside out, while soft-ripened cheeses age from the outside in. Once a cheese is cut, it begins to deteriorate. Buy cheese in quantities that can be eaten in a short amount of time, within a day or two for soft, fresh cheeses and within a week or two for aged cheeses after they've been cut.

The rind is the skin; it protects what's inside. Just as the flavors of wine develop quite rapidly once the cork is pulled, so do the flavors of cheese begin to change as soon as the paste is exposed to air. Once you cut the rind, you'll have a limited time in which to enjoy that cheese.

Tips for keeping your cheese in top condition

- Aged or grating cheeses have a low moisture content, which enables them to keep longer than soft and fresh cheeses. Fresh and soft cheeses should be eaten shortly after you buy them.

- The dry, forced airflow in your refrigerator can rob a cheese of moisture, which causes a loss of flavor and texture. Keep your cheese in the vegetable crisper compartment of the refrigerator. Serious cheese fans may want to invest in a cheese safe, which is a small wooden container that helps maintain a cheese-happy environment.

- If you introduce a little moisture to the contained area where you keep your cheeses, it will slow down dehydration. This can be as easy as putting a damp towel in the box with the cheese. The towel should be damp, not soaking wet; the last thing you want is to have your beautiful cheese sitting in a pool of water.

- Wrap your cheese in wax paper or butcher paper. Often retailers wrap cheese in plastic wrap. Take off that plastic, then rewrap your cheese. Paper allows a cheese to breathe and expel moisture, whereas plastic wrap can trap too much moisture, which affects the cheese's texture and flavor over time. Plastic wrap can also impart its own flavor to the cheese, which you don't want.

- Cheese tastes best when it's not cold from the fridge because the subtle nuances of flavor increase dramatically as the cheese comes closer to room temperature. When ready to serve a piece of cheese, take it out of the refrigerator early enough so the cheese can come to room temperature. In hot weather, one hour is usually enough time; in cool weather, three hours ahead of time may be better.

- Just before you set out a cheese for guests (or for yourself), lightly scrape the face of the cheese with a sharp paring knife. This will help eliminate surface oils and off-flavors resulting from oxidation.

- Don't throw away cheese. Most of us who love cheese end up with ends and bits in the cheese area of the fridge. Although these may not be suitable for a cheese board, we've come up with some good ways to use them, as you'll see in the next few pages.

- Singing to your cheeses may not extend their life, but it will definitely start every cheese tasting off in the right spirit.

RUSTIC CHEESE AND ONION GALETTES, TWO WAYS

MAKES ONE 8-IN/20-CM GALETTE; SERVES 4 AS AN APPETIZER

A flaky, buttery galette makes a fine starting point for using the ends and bits of cheese in your fridge. You can top these with almost any kind of grating cheese. Two kinds of cheese are better than one. Here we made a galette with onion, bacon, Ossau, and Vella Dry Jack, and then we made a second version with onion, fresh ricotta, lots of herbs, and paper-thin slices of lemon. You could also use this same dough for a sweeter galette made with mascarpone and fresh berries or stone fruit.

Make sure the butter is very cold before you start. Don't roll the dough; use your hands to press it into a round. Don't use a stand mixer or any mixer with this dough; you want small butter chips throughout because they're what make the galette so tender and flaky. Make this dough ahead if you like: Form it into a disk, wrap securely in plastic wrap, and then refrigerate for a day or two. Give the dough at least 1 hour to come to room temperature when you're ready to shape the galettes.

We say 1 tbsp of grated cheese below, but that's not really how we do it. Just grate the cheese directly over the galette without measuring and suit your own tastes.

Galette Dough

U.S.		METRIC
2 cups	All-purpose flour	255 g
Pinch	Sea salt	Pinch
¾ cup	Unsalted butter, very cold	170 g
4 tbsp	Cold water	4 tbsp
1	Egg yolk	1

Ossau and Dry Jack Galette

U.S.		METRIC
½	Yellow onion, thinly sliced into half-moons, sautéed in 1 tbsp unsalted butter	½
1 tbsp	Grated Ossau or any grating cheese	1 tbsp
1 tbsp	Grated Vella Dry Jack cheese	1 tbsp
1 tbsp	Grated Parmesan or Grana Padano cheese (see headnote)	1 tbsp
1 slice	Bacon, cooked crisp and chopped	1 slice

continued

	Ricotta, Herb, and Lemon Galette	
U.S.		METRIC
½	Yellow onion, thinly sliced into half-moons, sautéed in 1 tbsp unsalted butter	½
1	Small lemon (preferably Meyer), sliced paper-thin	1
4 tsp	Fresh ricotta cheese	4 tsp
1 tbsp	Chopped fresh flat-leaf parsley	1 tbsp
2 tsp	Chopped fresh basil, lemon thyme, or any fresh herb	2 tsp

To make the dough: Combine the flour and salt in a bowl. Using a pastry blender or your fingers, cut half of the butter into the dry ingredients until the mixture looks like coarse meal. Cut in the remaining butter until the butter is the size of peas. Drizzle on 3 tbsp of the cold water and stir just until moistened. Gather up the dough and knead it just a few times until it holds together. Flatten the dough into a disk, wrap in plastic wrap, and refrigerate for at least 30 minutes.

When the dough has chilled, shape it into a round with your hands. Don't overwork it. Transfer it to a baking sheet lined with parchment paper. Form the rim of the crust by gently lifting a small section of dough and pressing it inward. Mix the egg yolk with the remaining 1 tbsp water to make an egg wash. Set it aside.

Preheat the oven to 400°F/200°C/gas 6.

To make the Ossau and Dry Jack Galette: Spread the sautéed onion over the dough. Sprinkle the grated Ossau, Jack, and Parmesan over the onion. Scatter the bacon on top. With a pastry brush, moisten the crust rim all the way around with the egg wash. Bake until the pastry turns golden brown, 15 to 20 minutes. Slide the galette onto a wire rack and let cool for 10 minutes. Cut into wedges and serve.

To make the Ricotta, Herb, and Lemon Galette: Spread the sautéed onion over the dough. Arrange the lemon slices evenly over the onion. Drop small spoonfuls of the ricotta over the onion and lemon slices. With a pastry brush, moisten the crust rim all the way around with the egg wash. Bake until the pastry turns golden brown, 15 to 20 minutes. Slide the galette onto a wire rack and let cool for 10 minutes. Sprinkle the herbs over the top, cut into wedges, and serve.

PENNE WITH GREEN GARLIC FRESH CHEESE SAUCE

SERVES 6 TO 8

This mac and cheese has the flavor of lasagna but is lighter and fresher tasting, thanks to green garlic and fresh herbs.

Sue learned this trick of puréeing cottage cheese in a blender from one of our regular farmers' market customers. Blend the cottage cheese in your blender first, by itself, until smooth. Then pour in the milk and crème fraîche. This is so easy it's hard to believe how good it makes a mac and cheese.

U.S.		METRIC
8 oz	Cottage cheese	225 g
8 oz	Crème fraîche	240 ml
8 oz	Whole milk	240 ml
1 lb	Penne	455 g
1 tbsp	Unsalted butter	1 tbsp
2½ cups	Chopped fresh tomatoes	500 g
2 tbsp	Olive oil	2 tbsp
1 cup	Diced spring onions	150 g
1 cup	Diced green garlic	135 g
1 tbsp	Red pepper flakes	1 tbsp
2 tbsp	Minced fresh flat-leaf parsley	2 tbsp
2 tbsp	Minced fresh chives	2 tbsp
1 tsp	Sea salt	1 tsp
1 lb	Grated ends and bits of cheese, such as Dry Jack	455 g

Bring a large pot of water to a boil.

While the water heats, purée the cottage cheese in a blender on high speed until smooth, about 1 minute. Pour in the crème fraîche and milk and blend just until combined. Set the mixture aside.

When the water boils, add the penne. Don't overcook it; drain the pasta when it's just al dente. Spoon the cooked pasta into a 14-in/35.5-cm round baking dish or a 13-by-9-in/33-by-23-cm baking dish, and toss with the butter. Set the pan of pasta aside.

Pour the chopped tomatoes into a strainer and set aside to drain. You don't need to reserve the juice.

continued

Heat a medium saucepan over medium-high heat. When the pan is hot, add the olive oil. Add the spring onions and green garlic and cook just until translucent, about 2 minutes. Add the drained tomatoes and cook until the tomatoes are soft and there's not much juice in the pan, about 8 minutes. Add the red pepper flakes, parsley, chives, and salt; stir and then transfer the tomato-herb mixture into the pan with the buttered pasta. Stir the grated cheese into the cottage cheese–milk mixture, then pour into the pan and stir again. Stir in half of the grated cheese and pat the pasta smooth with the back of a spoon. Sprinkle the remaining cheese over the top and bake until the top is browned and bubbly, about 40 minutes. Let cool for 10 to 15 minutes before serving.

CLASSIC MAC AND CHEESE

SERVES 4

This version is creamy and simple, so the flavor of your cheese comes through. Choose a good sharp Cheddar as a base; you need 16 oz/455 g of cheese plus the Parmesan. You can use all Cheddar or a combination of half Cheddar and half ends and bits. Some folks add parsley or other herbs before baking (as shown in photo). We like to make it without herbs.

U.S.		METRIC
2 tbsp	Unsalted butter	2 tbsp
2 tbsp	All-purpose flour	2 tbsp
2½ cups	Whole milk	600 ml
¾ cup	Heavy cream	180 ml
1 tbsp	Dijon mustard	1 tbsp
1 lb	Grating cheese	455 g
¼ tsp	Sea salt	¼ tsp
	Freshly ground black pepper	
¼ tsp	Hot sauce	¼ tsp
12 oz	Pasta (elbow or corkscrew)	340 g
1½ cups	Panko or fresh bread crumbs (see page 241)	170 g
3 tbsp	Grated Parmesan or other cheese	3 tbsp

Preheat the oven to 400°F/200°C/gas 6. Place a rack in the bottom third of the oven, and butter a 3-qt/2.8-L baking dish. Set a large pot of unsalted water over high heat.

While the water heats, melt the butter in a large saucepan. When the butter has finished foaming, stir in the flour, whisking until the flour takes on a little color, about 3 minutes. Take the pan off the heat and pour in the milk slowly, while whisking continuously. Return the pan to medium heat. Stir until the mixture begins to thicken (about 5 minutes) and then take the pan off the heat again; stir in the cream, mustard, and three-fourths of the cheese. Stir in the salt, a few grinds of pepper, and the hot sauce. Set the sauce aside.

Cook the pasta just until al dente. Drain (don't rinse) and quickly stir the pasta into the cheese sauce, then pour into the prepared pan, scraping all the cheese sauce into the dish. Sprinkle the remaining grated cheese over the pasta. Sprinkle the panko over the cheese, and sprinkle the Parmesan on top of that.

Bake until the mixture is bubbling on the edges and showing some golden brown color on top, 25 to 35 minutes. Let the dish cool for at least 10 minutes before serving.

COWGIRLS' VERSION OF THE CLASSIC

SERVES 6 TO 8

This recipe features our own Wagon Wheel cheese. We like to make this with the wheel-shaped pasta called rotelle. Bacon makes it even better, as bacon always does.

U.S.		METRIC
1 tbsp	Kosher salt	1 tbsp
1 lb	Large rotelle pasta	455 g
8 tbsp	Unsalted butter	115 g
½ cup	All-purpose flour	60 g
4 cups	Whole milk, at room temperature	1 L
1½ lb	Coarsely shredded Wagon Wheel cheese	455 g
8 oz	Coarsely shredded sharp white Cheddar	225 g
5 slices	Bacon, diced, fried crisp, and drained	5 slices
½ tsp	Ground white pepper	½ tsp
½ tsp	Freshly ground nutmeg	½ tsp
½ tsp	Mustard powder (such as Colman's)	½ tsp
1 cup	Fresh bread crumbs (see page 241)	70 g
4	Medium red heirloom tomatoes, cored and sliced	4

Preheat the oven to 375°F/190°C/gas 5. Butter a 3-qt/2.8-L baking dish.

Bring an extra-large pot of water to boiling. Stir in the salt and rotelle. Cook the pasta until it's just shy of being tender, 6 to 7 minutes. Drain well.

In a large, heavy saucepan over medium heat, melt 6 tbsp/85 g of the butter. When the butter is bubbly and fragrant, whisk in the flour to form a smooth paste. Cook, whisking, until the mixture turns golden, 2 to 3 minutes. While still whisking, slowly pour in the milk. Whisk over the heat until the mixture thickens and bubbles, another 3 to 5 minutes. Remove from the heat.

continued

With a wooden spoon, stir in both cheeses, the bacon, pepper, nutmeg, and mustard powder. Add the cooked pasta; mix well but gently.

Melt the remaining 2 tbsp butter in a small pan, remove from the heat, and combine with the bread crumbs. Set aside.

Transfer the cheese mixture to the prepared baking dish. Arrange the sliced tomatoes in wagon-wheel fashion over the top of the pasta mixture. Sprinkle with the buttered bread crumbs.

Bake, uncovered, until the top is a nice golden brown and bubbling on the edges, 30 to 35 minutes. Let the dish cool for at least 10 minutes before serving.

GRUYÈRE WITH CAYENNE, CHOLULA, AND ELBOW MACARONI

SERVES 6 TO 8

Gruyère with Cholula is unexpected, but this combination is so good. Cholula is a hot sauce from Mexico that's worth seeking out, but regular Tabasco Sauce or Green Tabasco will work here, too. Choose fresh aromatic spices for the best flavor.

U.S.		METRIC
1 tbsp	Extra-virgin olive oil	1 tbsp
3 tbsp	Unsalted butter	3 tbsp
½ cup	Finely chopped yellow onion	75 g
¼ tsp	Ground New Mexico red chile	¼ tsp
Pinch	Cayenne pepper	Pinch
½ tsp	Cholula or Tabasco Sauce	½ tsp
1 lb	Elbow macaroni	455 g

Cheese sauce

U.S.		METRIC
4 tbsp	Unsalted butter	55 g
2 tbsp	All-purpose flour	2 tbsp
2 cups	Whole milk or half-and-half	480 ml
1 lb	Gruyère cheese, grated	455 g
¼ tsp	Sea salt	¼ tsp
1 tsp	Freshly ground black pepper	1 tsp
2 tbsp	Finely chopped fresh cilantro	2 tbsp
1½ tbsp	Sherry vinegar	1½ tbsp
¼ cup	Fresh bread crumbs (see page 241) or panko	30 g

Bring a large pot of water to a boil.

Heat a large saucepan over medium-high heat. Add the olive oil and 1 tbsp of the butter. When the butter is melted and hot, add the onion. Cook until the onion is soft—don't let it brown—and then add the ground chile, cayenne, and Cholula. Take the pan off the heat and set it aside.

continued

Preheat the oven to 375°F/190°C/gas 5.

When the water boils, add the macaroni. Don't overcook it; drain the pasta when it's just al dente. Spoon the cooked pasta into a 14-in/35.5-cm round baking dish or a 13-by-9-in/33-by-23-cm baking dish, and toss with the remaining 2 tbsp butter. Set the pan aside while you make the sauce.

To make the cheese sauce: Add 2 tbsp of the butter to a medium saucepan or skillet. (Don't use a nonstick pan.) When it's sizzling, add the flour and whisk constantly over medium heat until the mixture shows just a little color. Don't let it turn brown. Keep whisking while you slowly pour in the milk. It's fine if the butter and flour seize up when you add the liquid, just keep whisking. Let the mixture thicken slightly, and then stir in the Gruyère, salt, pepper, cilantro, and sherry vinegar. Pour the mixture over the pasta in the pan. Sprinkle the bread crumbs over the top of the pasta. Cut the remaining 2 tbsp butter into tiny pieces and dot over the pasta.

Cook until bubbly around the edges and browned on top, about 50 minutes. Let cool for 10 to 15 minutes before serving.

GRILLED CHEESE SANDWICHES, FOUR WAYS

Glorious grilled cheese sandwiches are appropriate whenever you need a little love. We make hundreds of grilled cheese sandwiches every day at our three cheese shops. Over the years we've learned a thing or two.

Having Steve and Suzie Sullivan and their Acme Bread store right beside our store in the Ferry Building is a reminder that we have old friends in the business. Acme Bread, Peet's Coffee, McEvoy Olive Oil, and the Cowgirls were the first four businesses to sign leases at the Ferry Building, and we were able to pick the space we wanted. Having the bread store beside the cheese store worked for us on a few levels.

This story tells you something about the Sullivans. During their honeymoon in France, Steve and Suzie visited the Peyraud family at Domaine Tempier in Bandol. While talking about the similarities between breadbaking and winemaking, one of the Peyrauds suggested that Steve make a levain—a wild yeast starter for bread—from the wild yeasts that gather on grapes in a vineyard. That idea stayed with Steve, and when he returned home to California, he raided the half-dozen grapevines in his father's backyard, tied the grapes up in cheesecloth, and immersed the bundle in a flour-water slurry, bashing it around a bit to release the grape juices. Within a day, the mixture had become an extremely active culture, which Steve used to make his delicious naturally leavened bread.

Peggy remembers working with Steve at Chez Panisse before he started Acme, when he made all the bread for the upstairs café and the downstairs restaurant. There were three ovens in which Steve baked the bread, and Peg remembers Steve timing his baking almost to the second, putting the bread in each oven sequentially, running up and downstairs with a spritz bottle in hand, and then the *spritz spritz spritz* sound as he monitored the heat, pulling out the fragrant loaves the minute they were done. Everybody who cooked downstairs wanted to munch those loaves, so Steve had to hide the bread to keep it safe.

When Steve and Suzie founded Acme Bread, they set an example that resonated. The Sullivans showed us there were other avenues to pursue besides opening restaurants. They worked so hard on an everyday food—Steve on the bread and Suzie on every other part of their business. By making their bread far better than any other bread sold at that time, they paved the way for many good bakers as well as other types of artisanal food producers in the Bay Area and across the country.

Steve's brother, Michael Sullivan, who's a wine importer, was a good friend as well from the many Vinexpos we attended together. Michael and his wife, Sylvie, focused on the Burgundy region in France and brought in many fine wines from small producers. We joke that with the Sullivans and the Cowgirls, you can put together a really good picnic.

For us, there's the bigger picture of food sources such as Acme Bread that you know are made with care, with organic ingredients, and with integrity. But when you taste Steve's bread, you're not thinking of any of that. You're just thinking about how good it tastes.

Having the Sullivans working next door, seeing their daughters Rebecca and Rachel grow up, and even seeing the next generation of bakers—Rebecca's daughter Dia—gives us faith about the artisan food producers still coming up.

continued

SIMPLE, CLASSIC GRILLED CHEESE

MAKES 3 SANDWICHES

This may be the one best way to use up the cheese ends and bits in your fridge. You can make this with almost any cheese and be completely satisfied.

U.S.		METRIC
4 oz	Fromage blanc	115 g
4 oz	Cheddar cheese (or any cheese), grated	115 g
4 oz	Monterey Jack (or any cheese), grated	115 g
6 slices	Levain bread (from Acme Bread, if you're lucky)	6 slices
2 tbsp	Unsalted butter	2 tbsp

In a medium bowl, combine all three cheeses. Divide the cheese mixture evenly between three slices of the bread, top with the remaining three bread slices to form sandwiches, and butter the outside of the bread.

Heat a well-seasoned cast-iron skillet or any large pan with a heavy bottom over medium heat.

Place a sandwich in the heated pan and cook until the bread touching the pan is golden brown, 5 to 7 minutes. Flip the sandwich and continue to cook until the cheese is completely melted and the bottom of the sandwich is golden brown. Repeat for each sandwich and serve right away.

continued

CHERYL'S GRILLED CHEESE WITH
CARAMELIZED ONIONS AND PEARS
MAKES 3 SANDWICHES

Caramelizing diced pear along with the onion gives this sandwich a hint of sweetness that works well with the rich flavors of the cheese. If you don't have pears, caramelize the onion by itself and slather a thick layer of fig preserves onto the bread before you add the cheese and grill the sandwich.

Cheryl Dobbins, who leads tours of our Point Reyes cheesemaking rooms every Friday, once owned her own bakery, The Cherry Street Bakery in Tulsa, Oklahoma, so she has firm ideas about what makes a good sandwich. This one is really good. Once you try this one, it'll be a permanent addition to your grilled cheese repertoire.

U.S.		METRIC
3 tbsp	Unsalted butter	3 tbsp
1 tbsp	Extra-virgin olive oil	1 tbsp
1 cup	Medium-diced yellow onion	230 g
1 cup	Peeled, seeded, and diced pear (preferably Comice or Asian pear)	260 g
	Sea salt and freshly ground black pepper	
8 oz	Medium-grated semisoft cheese (such as Gruyère, Cheddar, Wagon Wheel, Monterey Jack)	225 g
4 oz	Fromage blanc	115 g
6 slices	Soft bread, such as potato bread	6 slices
1 tsp	Dijon mustard (optional)	1 tsp

In a medium sauté pan, heat 1 tbsp of the butter with the olive oil over medium heat. When the butter is bubbling, add the onion and the pear to the pan. Cook over medium heat, stirring often, until the onion and pear are translucent and browned, 5 to 7 minutes. Add a pinch of salt and pepper, remove the pan from the heat, and set it aside to cool.

In a mixing bowl, combine the two cheeses. When the onion-pear mixture is cool, add it to the cheese. (Wait until the onion-pear mixture is barely warm; if it's mixed in when hot, the cheese will melt and clump, causing it to cook unevenly.)

Spread the cheese mixture on one side of each of three bread slices. Spread the Dijon mustard (if you like mustard; if not, leave it out) on the remaining bread slices and place mustard-side down on the cheese mixture to make sandwiches. Butter the outside of each sandwich on both sides with the remaining 2 tbsp butter.

Heat a well-seasoned cast-iron skillet or any large pan with a heavy bottom over medium heat.

Place a sandwich in the heated pan and cook until the bread touching the pan is golden brown, 5 to 7 minutes. Flip the sandwich and continue to cook until the cheese is completely melted and the bottom of the sandwich is golden brown. Repeat for each sandwich and serve right away.

continued

NAN'S GRILLED MOZZARELLA AND OLIVE SALAD SANDWICH
MAKES 4 SANDWICHES

Every year we head to New Orleans for the Jazz Festival, and every year we make a stop at Central Market Grocery for olive salad. Our version is more coarsely chopped so you get big, juicy chunks of olive, and we've brightened it up with orange juice and zest.

Nan Haynes, who did many of the grocery runs while we developed the recipes for this book, is one of those olive people who can't walk past a gourmet olive bar without filling a few tubs to take home. Thanks to Nan, we made this salad with several different varieties of green olives—Picholine, Sevillano, Manzanilla—and liked every single version.

Olives with pits taste much better than pitted olives from a can. Pitting olives is easy. Lay the flat of a chef's knife on the olive and, with your hand, gently smash the olive, which should then loosen its hold on the pit.

Olive Salad

U.S.		METRIC
1½ cups	Pitted green olives, coarsely chopped	180 g
½ cup	Pitted kalamata olives, coarsely chopped	60 g
1 tbsp	Drained capers	1 tbsp
2	Garlic cloves, sliced	2
¼ cup	Thinly sliced celery	30 g
1 tbsp	Coarsely chopped fresh flat-leaf parsley	1 tbsp
¼ cup	Red wine vinegar	60 ml
½ cup	Olive oil	120 ml
¼ cup	Freshly squeezed orange juice	60 ml
1 tsp	Freshly grated orange zest	1 tsp
1 tsp	Red pepper flakes	1 tsp
½ lb	Fresh mozzarella	225 g
8 slices	Levain or olive bread, cut ½ in/12 mm thick	8 slices
2 tbsp	Unsalted butter	2 tbsp

To make the olive salad: Mix together the chopped olives in a medium bowl. Add the capers, garlic, celery, and parsley; stir. Pour in the vinegar, olive oil, orange juice, orange zest, and red pepper flakes; stir. This will keep covered in the refrigerator for 3 days.

Divide the mozzarella evenly between four slices of the bread. Divide the olive salad into four equal portions, spooning one portion over each mozzarella-topped bread slice. Top with the remaining bread slices to make four sandwiches, and butter the outside of each sandwich.

Heat a well-seasoned cast-iron skillet or any large pan with a heavy bottom over medium heat.

Place a sandwich in the heated pan and cook until the bread touching the pan is golden brown, 5 to 7 minutes.

Flip the sandwich and continue to cook until the cheese is completely melted and the bottom of the sandwich is golden brown. Repeat for each sandwich and serve right away.

continued

KATE'S GRILLEY—STILTON AND CHESHIRE ON WALNUT BREAD
MAKES 3 SANDWICHES

We worked with Kate Arding for several years when we opened Cowgirl Creamery, and her English style continues to influence our work today. Being from Kent, Kate has a distinct voice and accent that has resonated through the American cheese world.

Knowing how she adores grilled cheese sandwiches—which she lovingly refers to as grilleys—we dedicate this very British version to her.

U.S.		METRIC
4 oz	Fromage blanc	115 g
4 oz	Wagon Wheel (or Fontina or a young Asiago) cheese, grated	115 g
4 oz	Stilton, finely crumbled or grated	115 g
6 slices	Walnut bread	6 slices
2 tbsp	Unsalted butter	2 tbsp

In a medium bowl, combine all three cheeses. Divide the cheese mixture evenly between three slices of the bread, top with the remaining three bread slices to form sandwiches, and butter the outside of the bread.

Heat a well-seasoned cast-iron skillet or any large pan with a heavy bottom over medium heat.

Place a sandwich in the heated pan and cook until the bread touching the pan is golden brown, 5 to 7 minutes.

Flip the sandwich and continue to cook until the cheese is completely melted and the bottom of the sandwich is golden brown. Repeat for each sandwich and serve right away.

COWGIRLS' TIPS FOR
GREAT GRILLED CHEESE SANDWICHES

- The best-tasting sandwiches combine three cheeses. For a creamier cheese middle, make one of them a soft cheese such as fromage blanc. This acts as a suspension; just as egg whites suspend the heavier particles in a soufflé, so does the soft cheese suspend the grated cheese and distribute it more evenly across the bread. The end result is a much creamier filling.

- Think about pairing cheeses to complement texture. For example, if one of the cheeses you're using is hard, such as Parmesan, use another cheese that's more elastic, such as mozzarella.

- Find a bread that enhances your sandwiches. We like baguettes or levain, but use your favorite bread. Bread that is slightly stale is better; because it's not as moist, it browns better.

- Use regular butter, not clarified butter. At Sidekick, our lunch counter in the Ferry Building in San Francisco, we started out using clarified butter but found that regular butter made tastier sandwiches. Those milk solids add to the flavor.

- Use a well-seasoned cast-iron skillet or any large pan with a heavy bottom. Set your pan over medium-low to medium heat. Because you're cooking with regular butter, you don't want a too-hot pan, or the butter will burn.

- Don't skimp on the cheese; use a good amount. It's okay if the cheese filling spills out onto the hot pan. Those crunchy cheese bits around the edge of the sandwich are always welcome.

- Cooking a grilled cheese takes longer than you'd expect. Count on at least 3 minutes on each side.

SIDEKICK TOMATO SOUP

SERVES 8 TO 10

This soup is called Sidekick because it is the best sidekick to a grilled cheese sandwich. On the menu at our lunch counter in the San Francisco Ferry Building, also called Sidekick, it has many loyal fans. This soup relies on great tomatoes. We use canned organic San Marzano tomatoes from Italy. A big Cowgirl "thank you" to all the customers over the years who've asked us for this recipe.

U.S.		METRIC
2 tbsp	Extra-virgin olive oil	2 tbsp
1	Large yellow onion, finely diced	1
2	Large carrots, finely diced	2
2	Large garlic cloves, minced	2
1½ tsp	Dried oregano	1½ tsp
¼ tsp	Red pepper flakes	¼ tsp
2	Bay leaves	2
1½ tsp	Kosher salt	1½ tsp
Two 16-oz	Cans organic tomatoes	Two 480-ml
2 cups	Water	480 ml
2 tbsp	Finely minced fresh rosemary	2 tbsp
1 tbsp	Finely minced fresh basil	1 tbsp
1 cup	Crème fraîche, for garnish	240 ml

Put a large stockpot over medium-high heat. Pour in the olive oil and allow it to heat. Add the onion, carrots, garlic, oregano, red pepper flakes, and bay leaves, plus 1 tsp of the salt. Cook, stirring occasionally, until the vegetables have softened and the onion is translucent, 6 to 8 minutes.

Add the tomatoes plus two cans of water. Bring the liquid to a simmer and then decrease the heat to medium-low. Add half of the minced rosemary and basil and simmer the soup over very low heat for about 2 hours. During the last 20 minutes of cooking, add the remaining minced rosemary and basil and the remaining ½ tsp salt.

Use an immersion blender to make the mixture smooth; alternately, purée the soup in a standard blender, in batches, if necessary. Strain the soup through a fine-holed china cap, medium-mesh strainer, or chinois, pressing the solids with a wooden spoon to extract as much liquid as you can. (Taste the soup and add more salt or minced rosemary or basil, if needed.)

Garnish with the crème fraîche and serve warm.

PARMESAN BROTH

10 CUPS/2.4 L

You can make a delicious, full-flavored stock from the leftover bits of hard cheese and pieces of natural rinds found in the cheese corner of your refrigerator. Mushroom and the cheeses give this stock a deep, earthy flavor. We make this often, as it's a wonderful starting point for soups and sauces.

You can add leftover cheese bits to any other stock also, but if you try this recipe, you might be surprised by how well this stock compares with chicken or beef stock. Save your cheese rinds and bits in the fridge until you have about 1 cup/200 g full. Before starting the stock, clean the cheeses by slicing off any unknown molds. Parmesan and Cheddar rinds taste wonderful in this stock but any natural rind that is not too crumbly can work well.

U.S.		METRIC
12 cups	Cool water	2.8 L
1 tbsp	Unsalted butter	1 tbsp
2 cups	Medium-diced onions	300 g
1 cup	Coarsely chopped carrots	135 g
1 cup	Coarsely chopped celery	115 g
¼ oz	Dried mushrooms, such as porcini or shiitake	7 g
2	Bay leaves	2
3 sprigs	Fresh thyme	3 sprigs
3 sprigs	Fresh flat-leaf parsley	3 sprigs
About 1 cup	Leftover bits of hard cheese and natural rinds	About 200 g

In a large pot, bring the water to a simmer over medium-high heat.

While the water heats, in another large pot, melt the butter over medium heat. When it's melted, add the onions, carrots, celery, mushrooms, bay leaves, thyme, and parsley. Cook until the onions are translucent and the carrots, celery, and mushrooms are soft, about 8 minutes. With a wooden spoon, stir in the cheese bits. Let the cheese and vegetables sit on the bottom of the pot for short periods of time, no longer than 10 seconds; this will allow the vegetables and the cheese to brown the bottom of the pot a little. (You don't want all the vegetables browned, but just the bottom surface needs a little color.) Stir often.

When the vegetables and cheese at the very bottom of the pot show some brown and the cheese is beginning to melt, slowly introduce the simmering water to the pot, stirring in just 1 cup/240 ml to start. Stirring constantly, deglaze the pan's bottom with the hot water to loosen any browned bits. When the pot bottom is clean of any brown, pour in the remainder of the water. Decrease the heat to medium-low and monitor the heat, adjusting the flame so the broth stays at a gentle simmer.

Simmer for 40 to 50 minutes, stirring every 3 to 5 minutes, so the broth doesn't pick up a scorched flavor. Strain the broth into a very large container or another clean pot and allow it to cool. Once it's cool, you can easily skim the top of any fats. Store this in your refrigerator for up to 3 days or in your freezer for up to 3 months.

COWGIRL KITCHEN TECHNIQUES

THESE ARE TECHNIQUES THAT WE'VE LEARNED over years and years of restaurant cooking. These can make your time in the kitchen more efficient. You'll use these techniques in recipes throughout this book.

PREPARING ANCHOVIES

The anchovies packed in oil that you find at the supermarket can have a strong fishy flavor and be on the mushy side. We prefer imported salt-packed anchovies, which taste cleaner and sweeter than oil-packed. Rinse these in cool water before using.

If you have anchovies with bones, remove the bones by slipping your finger between the spine and the fillet, and running your finger along the length of the fish to loosen the skeleton. Then lift out the bones (intact if you're careful), throw the bones away, and use the fillets as needed. Store any leftover tinned anchovies in a container with a tight cover.

BLANCHING ASPARAGUS

Many people like to dunk their asparagus in ice water as soon as it comes from the pot. We prefer to blanch the stalks until they're not quite as tender as you'd like them to be. Taste while you blanch, and watch the vegetable's color: when it turns bright green, take a stalk from the pot and taste. If it's almost tender with just a hint of crispness, it's ready.

As soon as you take the stalks from the water, dry them quickly with a paper towel or clean kitchen towel and then dress them with extra-virgin olive oil, salt, and pepper. The asparagus absorbs the seasonings better if you do this while the stalks are still warm.

Very fat asparagus can sometimes have a woody stem. Use a vegetable peeler to lightly peel off the skin just from the point where the stalks seem woody.

MAKING A VINAIGRETTE

A standard vinaigrette is simply three parts oil to one part vinegar, but you'll vary this proportion quite a bit depending on whether your oil is heavier tasting or your vinegar more acidic. Tasting is critical as you pour in more oil or acid. You'll want to pull out your very best oils and vinegars when you make a vinaigrette because this is where you can really taste an oil's or a vinegar's flavors.

We believe the best vinaigrettes contain a combination of vinegars. For example, if you combine sherry vinegar and balsamic vinegar, the sherry vinegar adds brightness while the balsamic or wine vinegar contributes a richer, more mellow flavor.

The other trick we use when making dressings is to finely dice shallots, and then macerate the dice in the mixed vinegars for about 10 minutes before adding oil or other dressing ingredients. The shallot bits absorb the vinegar and release a bright note of flavor in the mouth.

MAKING BREAD CRUMBS

Good bread crumbs rely on good bread, and bread crumbs made at home taste so much fresher and lighter than those you can buy.

When you have leftover good bread that's gotten stale, cut the bread into slices and then cubes. Preheat the oven to 300°F/150°C/gas 2.

Grind the bread cubes in a blender or a food processor. (A blender will give you a slightly more even crumb.) Spread the crumbs evenly on a baking sheet and toast in the oven. Watch closely; as soon as the crumbs begin to show a faint hint of color, take the pan out of the oven and remove the crumbs from the pan to cool. When cool, store crumbs in ziplock plastic bags. They'll keep in your refrigerator for up to 1 week.

For garlic bread crumbs: Preheat the oven to 350°F/180°C/gas 4. Cut the stale bread into slices and arrange them on a baking sheet. Bake until they turn light brown, about 7 minutes. While the slices are still warm, rub each side with the cut edge of a garlic clove. Set the slices aside to cool completely. When they're cool, break the bread into pieces and grind in batches in a blender or food processor. If not using right away, seal the crumbs in ziplock plastic bags and store in the refrigerator for up to 1 week.

USING THE WET-HAND/DRY-HAND METHOD OF BREADING

Whether dredging a squash blossom in cornmeal (see page 192) or a chicken paillard in grated Parmesan (see page 180), you can avoid lumps and missed spots by always using the same hand for dipping in the egg wash, and always using the other hand for dredging the egg-dunked item in the dry ingredient. It seems to be automatic to use the same hand for both tasks, but if you train yourself to keep one hand wet and one hand dry, anything you dip in flour, cornmeal, grated cheese, or bread crumbs will turn out more evenly coated.

CLARIFYING BUTTER

Clarified butter is regular butter that is heated and left to sit undisturbed so the milk fats settle at the bottom of the pan. The foamy solids are strained away, leaving a golden liquid that lets you cook at a slightly higher temperature than normal melted butter because the milk fat solids are what burn first.

To clarify butter: Cut butter into 1-in/2.5-cm chunks and place the chunks in a small heavy saucepan. Over low heat, melt the butter. Take it off the heat as soon as the butter is completely melted. Do not stir or swirl the pan. Let the butter cool in the pan for 3 to 6 minutes. Slowly pour the clear, golden clarified butter through a fine-mesh strainer into a clean glass jar, leaving the creamy solids in the bottom of the pan. Discard what's left in the pan. Clarified butter will keep for weeks in the refrigerator.

MAKING AND STORING COMPOUND BUTTER

As you can see on page 53, a compound butter is simply softened butter into which you've beaten herbs, spices, shallots, anchovies, or any number of flavorful or aromatic ingredients. After combining the butter and add-ins, spoon the mixture onto a sheet of wax paper. With your hands outside the paper, use the paper to roll up the butter into a cylinder about the size and shape of store-bought cookie dough (you'll form a log of butter wrapped in the wax paper). Twist each end of the wax paper tightly to seal, and then either store in a ziplock bag or wrap in plastic wrap to prevent the butter from absorbing any freezer odors.

COOKING WITH EGGS

If you crack open a supermarket egg and compare it to an egg just two or three days from the coop, you'll see a big difference. The yolks in farm-fresh eggs generally have a bolder, deeper color. You can taste the difference, too. Seek out fresh eggs at farmers' markets whenever you can.

Peggy feels strongly that food looks better without the "cords" in whole eggs (the tiny opaque part that is not yolk and not white), so they should be pulled out of raw eggs before you cook with them. Crack open raw eggs into a small bowl. With your fingers, remove the cords, discard them, and then use the eggs.

ROASTING GARLIC

To roast garlic: Preheat the oven to 400°F/200°C/gas 6. Wrap as many unpeeled garlic cloves as you want to roast in aluminum foil, creating a packet. It's best to roast at least 12 cloves.

Cook the cloves until they're soft and squishy to the touch, about 20 minutes. Let the cloves cool for 30 minutes to 1 hour, then peel the cloves or squeeze out the garlic with your fingers and discard the peels.

Then you can mash the garlic with a fork or with a mortar and pestle, with a few grains of salt, to create a fine paste. If you don't want to use this right away, spoon the garlic paste into an air-tight container and cover with a thin layer of olive oil. This will keep in your refrigerator for weeks.

PREPARING AN HERB CHIFFONADE

A chiffonade is a precise method of slicing that produces fine, thin ribbons. We most often slice a basil chiffonade, but you can use this technique with any herb that has good-size leaves. Stack washed leaves so each leaf's spine faces downward and all the leaf tips point in the same direction. Roll the stack of leaves like a cigar, starting from one side. Slice across the roll, perpendicular to the leaf's spine, cutting the leaves into fine ribbons.

FORMING A PIPING CONE OUT OF PAPER

If you don't have a pastry bag with which to fill the gougères (see page 143), it's easy to make a squeezable cone out of wax paper or parchment paper as a substitute. Just cut a sheet of paper 8 to 10 in/20 to 25 cm by 16 in/40 cm long. Roll it into a cone, starting at one corner. Spoon in whatever you'd like to pipe. Fold down the wide end—the top of the cone—and tape the fold in place. With scissors, trim off just a tiny smidge from the cone's tip and test the piping by squeezing onto a plate or paper. If the flow is too slow, cut a little more paper off the cone's tip.

You can fold the cone's tip and use it to store any leftover filling in your refrigerator. Once you've squeezed out all the contents, just throw the cone away.

MASTERING BÉCHAMEL

MAKES ABOUT 1½ CUPS/360 ML

A classic béchamel is a milk sauce that uses a simple mixture of butter and flour as a thickening agent. We use béchamel often.

Making a good béchamel is a matter of stirring or whisking a mixture steadily over heat until the butter-flour mixture has a little color but hasn't turned dark. Aim for a golden color just a little darker than butter. Another tip for success with béchamel is to first heat the milk in a separate small saucepan, and then take it off the heat, and have it nearby already warm, before you begin melting the butter.

Once you feel confident making béchamel, you'll use it in soufflés, mac and cheese, lasagnas, in sauces for fish, and in many other dishes.

U.S.		METRIC
1 to 1½ cups	Whole milk	240 to 360 ml
2 tbsp	Unsalted butter	2 tbsp
2 tbsp	All-purpose flour	2 tbsp
¼ tsp	Sea salt	¼ tsp
⅛ tsp	Black or white pepper	⅛ tsp

Warm the milk over low heat in a small saucepan. When it begins to show small bubbles, turn off the heat. In another saucepan over medium heat, melt the butter. When it's melted and the foaming has subsided, stir in the flour. Keep stirring until the flour begins to darken just slightly, about 2 minutes. Take it off the heat when it's about the color of butter. Let the mixture cool for 30 seconds.

Whisking the butter-flour mixture vigorously, pour in 1 cup/240 ml of the hot milk. Increase the heat to medium-high and keep whisking, getting the whisk into the sides of the pan. Whisk for 2 to 3 minutes; if the béchamel begins to boil too rapidly, pour in the remaining milk, a little at a time. When it's thick enough to coat a spoon, turn off the heat and whisk in the salt and pepper.

If not using the béchamel right away, cover it with plastic wrap, smoothing it across the surface of the sauce. This will keep in your refrigerator for 2 days.

THICK BÉCHAMEL

Make the béchamel richer by substituting half-and-half for the milk.

MORNAY SAUCE

This is a béchamel sauce to which you add ¼ cup/30 g of grated cheese, such as Parmesan or Gruyère, and a pinch of grated nutmeg at the very end, if you like.

STEEPING A VANILLA SYRUP

MAKES 5 CUPS/1.2 L

We use this for our Vanilla Egg Cream (page 45), but it's also delicious in lemonade and iced tea.

U.S.		METRIC
4 cups	Water	960 ml
2 lb	Sugar	910 g
2	Whole vanilla beans	2

Pour the water and sugar into a large pot. Bring to a boil over medium-high heat. Stir until the sugar is completely dissolved. Let the liquid boil gently for 1 minute more. Turn off the heat.

Halve the vanilla beans lengthwise and, with a knife, scrape out and reserve all the small black seeds inside the pods.

Add the seed scrapings and the vanilla bean pods to the sugar syrup, stir, and then let the vanilla steep while the syrup cools. When it's cool, remove and discard the vanilla pods.

Stored in jars or tightly corked bottles, the syrup will keep in your refrigerator for at least 6 months.

GLOSSARY

AFFINAGE

The craft of aging cheese in temperature- and humidity-controlled environments. Affinage may include washing with wine or any number of other additions to a cheese while it ages. Affinage can take place in spaces that allow the strict control of humidity and temperature to affect a certain outcome in a cheese, from limestone caves in Bordeaux (see page 62) to straw-bale aging rooms in Wisconsin (see page 38). This aging process partly determines the flavors found in individual cheeses.

AFFINEUR

A craftsperson who oversees the proper aging process of cheese. An affineur also determines whether further aging would be beneficial in creating a new flavor profile. The affineur (who might or might not be the original cheesemaker) decides when each cheese is ripe and ready to be released to market. They also possess the skills needed to introduce a new element to a cheese, such as herbing a cheese.

AOC (APPELLATION D'ORIGINE CONTRÔLÉE)

In France, this is the certification given to specific geographical regions for cheese, butter, wines, and other agricultural products. The AOC dates back to a fifteenth-century parliamentary decree that regulated Roquefort cheese, specifically what milk, region, and aging process were required for it to be called Roquefort. *See also* DOP.

BACTERIA

Specific, beneficial microorganisms that help transform milk into cheese can also account for particular flavors in the finished cheese. *Lactococcus lactis,* commonly known as lactic acid bacteria, ferments lactose (the sugars found in milk) into lactic acid.

BANDAGE-WRAPPED CHEESE

Strips of linen or cheesecloth wrapped around a cheese (traditionally, Cheddar) and then sealed in place with lard or butter. Wrapping a cheese protects it from unwanted bacteria while it ages. This may also be called linen-wrapped or clothbound.

BUTTERFAT

Because cheeses contain at least 50 percent water, which slowly disappears as the cheese dries or "dessicates," fat content constantly changes as the cheese slowly loses its moisture. Cheesemakers provide a more consistent fat measure through every stage of the cheese's aging by measuring the fat found in the cheese's solids, after the liquid is taken out of the equation. In the United States this measure is shown on cheese labels as IDM, which stands for "in dry matter." On French cheese labels, it's noted as m.g., which stands for "matière grasse."

CHEESE MITES

Microscopic organisms that feed on the rinds of certain cheeses. The mites are so small that you can't see them without magnification, but you can easily notice the residue they leave. Often found on natural-rind, aged cheeses such as Cheddar or Mimolette. Some cheesemakers posit the theory that mites are beneficial because they allow a limited amount of aeration that results in a superior cheese flavor.

CLABBER

An old-fashioned term used to describe cooked and cultured cream. We use clabber in our cottage cheese production. Traditionally it's made with raw milk set out so the cream rises to the top. Natural bacteria digest the lactose, converting it to lactose acid, which curdles the milk. We use pasteurized cream, so the cultures we introduce into the pasteurized milk are added for similar results.

COAGULANT

Certain enzymes react on very specific amino acids that make up the protein in milk. The reaction causes these components to bond, transforming a liquid (milk) into a gel (the first stage of cheese). Coagulants can be found in some plants such as nettles, cardoons, papaya, some mushrooms, and other fruits and vegetables. Coagulants can also be animal-based; rennet is an example. *See also* Rennet.

COOKED CURD

A cooked-curd cheese just means the curds and whey are heated to a temperature at which point the curd is gently cooked in the liquid whey.

COTTAGE CHEESE

All cottage cheese is made with skim milk. The curds, which are squeaky clean to start, require a dressing made of milk or cream to make the cottage cheese creamy.

CRÈME FRAÎCHE

Cream to which lactic acid is added. The lactic acid, which is often simply buttermilk, causes the cream to thicken over a period of hours.

CULTURES

See Starter Cultures.

DOP (DENOMINAZIONE DI ORIGINE PROTETTA)

From Italy, this is the certification given to specific geographical regions for cheese, butter, wines, and other agricultural products. Each product has to abide by a number of production regulations and geographical restrictions. This is similar to the French AOC but differs in that it's recognized by the European Union. *See also* AOC.

DOUBLE-CRÈME (OR DOUBLE-CREAM)

A measure of a cheese's butterfat. If a cheese's butterfat content measures between 60 percent and 74 percent, the cheese is labeled double-crème. *See also* Triple-Crème (or Triple-Cream).

DRYING OFF

A rest period in which a cow ceases to lactate, about three hundred days after giving birth. This happens naturally in most milking animals.

FRUITIÈRE

In the making of Comté in France, the cheesemaker to whom the farmers take milk is called a *fruitière*. Farmers generally live within eight miles/thirteen kilometres of their fruitière and deliver their milk every day. The fruitière, who normally makes cheese from the milk deliveries of eight to twenty farmers, follows the very strict rules in cheesemaking set by the Comté AOC. Not only is the fruitière obligated to follow the Comté's strict guidelines, but the farmers are also required to abide by rules concerning the breed of animal and how the animals are cared for. There are 175 Comté fruitières in all. *See also* AOC.

GEOTRICHUM CANDIDUM

Beneficial bacteria that aid in cheesemaking, affecting the flavor, texture, and character of a cheese as well as the rind's surface. Often bringing a slight odor of sulfur, this sturdy yeast works in conjunction with *Penicillium candidum* to discourage other stray microorganisms from growing on the rind. *See also Penicillium candidum.*

GREEN CHEESE

Formed unripe cheese. The affineur receives green cheese, oversees the aging process, and determines when the cheese is ripe and ready for market.

HOMOGENIZATION

A process that breaks the fat globules in milk into smaller particles in order to prevent separation. In milk that has not been homogenized, cream rises to the top.

HOOPING

When curd is placed into a cheese form. Most hoops are round, but cheese forms can be other shapes also.

IDM

On cheese labels, the IDM, or "in dry matter," measure refers to the fat content in just the solids of the cheese. To understand this more fully, see Butterfat.

INOCULATE

How cheesemakers add cultures to a vat of liquid milk as a step in cheesemaking. *See also* Starter Cultures.

LACTIC ACID

Just as there are beneficial microorganisms at work when you make bread, yogurt, beer, or wine, so are there helpful microbes at work in cheesemaking. *Lactococcus lactis*, commonly known as lactic acid bacteria, ferments lactose (the sugars found in milk) into lactic acid, which helps to transform liquid milk into solid cheese.

LACTIC ACID CHEESES

Generally fresh cheeses such as fromage blanc and quark that depend on lactic acid cultures for ripening and coagulation.

LINEN-WRAPPED CHEESE
See Bandage-Wrapped Cheese.

M.G.
On the labels of French cheeses, this notation—which stands for "matière grasse"—refers to the fat content in just the solids of the cheese. To understand this more fully, see Butterfat.

MESOPHILIC STARTER CULTURES
One of the most common strains of lactic acid bacteria used by cheesemakers, mesophilic cultures work in moderate heat and are slow acting. These are basically buttermilk cultures, so they often bring tart flavors with lemony notes to cheeses. *See also* Thermophilic Starter Cultures.

ORGANIC MILK
The United States Department of Agriculture (USDA) requires that food labels that use the word *organic* must be certified in accordance with our national standards. The whole idea behind certification is improving the health and well-being of the animals. Under the rules of certification, farmers cannot use growth hormones or antibiotics. Organic dairy farmers pay close attention to conditions that will reduce stress and prevent illness. The pasture that the animals graze on must be certified organic and any feed brought in to supplement the diet must be from sources that meet the national organic growing standards. These standards include limited use of pesticides, fertilizers, herbicides, and other toxic substances on the land with a focus on building the health of the soil, streams, and riparian corridors.

PASTE
The center of a cheese; everything encased in the rind.

PASTEURIZATION
Heating a food to a specific temperature in order to kill harmful bacteria.

PENICILLIUM CANDIDUM
A fungus or mold introduced in cheesemaking that helps create a fluffy white rinded cheese. *See also Geotrichum candidum.*

RAW MILK
Milk that has not been pasteurized. In the United States, it is legal to use raw milk in the production of cheeses that are aged over sixty days. *See also* Pasteurization.

RENNET
The addition of rennet encourages the protein molecules to bind evenly throughout the liquid milk, which means the curd sets more uniformly. Rennet is animal-based, found in the lining of the stomach of young mammals. Cheesemakers debate whether some vegetable-based coagulants can also be called rennet. Rennet is one of many coagulants that cheesemakers use. *See also* Coagulant.

RIND

A skin that forms around a cheese while it ages, protecting the inside of the cheese. Just as a wine once uncorked cannot continue to age, so a cheese once cut stops any beneficial flavor development. Once a cheese is opened, it must be consumed within a certain amount of time, depending on the type of cheese. Should you eat the rind? Depends on whom you ask. See "Ask the Cowgirls," page 75.

SOFT-RIPENED

A category of mold-ripened cheeses. Aging in a soft-ripened cheese takes place from the outside of the cheese, moving inward. Traditionally made with uncooked curd, these cheeses don't take long to ripen, but they have a short lifespan because the curd is so delicate. Examples include Brie and Camembert.

SOUR CREAM

Light cream that's been either cultured or acidified. Cultured sour cream is made by adding a culture that produces lactic acid, which thickens the cream. Acidified sour cream is made by adding an acid such as vinegar.

STARTER CULTURES

These are single strains of beneficial bacteria used by cheesemakers. Over centuries, cheesemakers have been able to isolate particular strains of bacteria that lead to specific changes during the process of transforming milk into cheese. By adding cultures to the liquid milk, cheesemakers affect the flavor and character of the finished product. *See also* Mesophilic Starter Cultures *and* Thermophilic Starter Cultures.

STRETCHED CURD

A cheese that is stretched and kneaded like a bread dough during cheesemaking when the curd reaches a specific pH level. This action is what gives mozzarella its elastic texture. The Italians call this *pasta filata*.

THERMOPHILIC STARTER CULTURES

One of the most common strains of lactic acid bacteria used by cheesemakers, thermophilic cultures work best in environments between 113°F/45°C and 252°F/122°C. *See also* Mesophilic Starter Cultures.

TRIPLE-CRÈME (OR TRIPLE-CREAM)

A measure of a cheese's butterfat. If a cheese's butterfat content measures more than 75 percent, the cheese is labeled triple-crème. *See also* Double-Crème (or Double-Cream).

YOGURT

Milk cultured with specific bacteria that produce lactic acid, which thickens the mixture and makes it tangy. Commercial yogurt makers may thicken the yogurt either through reverse osmosis or by adding thickeners such as tapioca (see page 43).

ACKNOWLEDGMENTS

Thanks to everyone who works with us at Cowgirl Creamery for their dedication in making, selling, and learning about cheese. There's no way we could have taken the time to write this book without the support of our entire Cowgirl family, especially Rachel Cohen, Ted Lin, Maureen Cunnie, Eric Patterson, and Debra Dickerson. We can't thank everyone affiliated with Cowgirl Creamery on this one page (or even in this one book), but we can thank those people who helped us tell our story.

Thanks to Bill LeBlond, who took us out for lunch at least once a year for the past eight years to encourage us to write this book. Thanks to our editor, Sarah Billingsley, for her careful eye, patience, and enthusiasm. Thanks to Sara Schneider for designing a beautiful, elegant book. Thanks to our thoughtful copyeditor Jane Horn.

Thanks to Ann Krueger Spivack, our in-house editor who spent many afternoons cooking with us in our home kitchens, taking notes, and formatting our recipes. Most important, she kept us on top of our deadlines and helped hone the text so that our two voices became one.

Thanks to our brainy and entertaining agent, Kitty Cowles, who helped develop the concept and the look of this book, and Dabney Gough, her colleague.

Thanks to Christopher Hirsheimer and Melissa Hamilton of Canal House, who always go the extra mile to get the best shot. Even without our words, their photographs tell a good story and make our recipes look so mouthwatering. Our time spent with the Canal House gals enriched our friendship and led us to some of the most beautiful places on Earth.

Thanks to Peggy Knickerbocker, who not only took the time to read our drafts and to comment without restraint but also contributed a couple of great recipes. Thanks to Albert Straus for sixteen years of great milk, and to the entire Straus family for being such an important part of our lives.

Thanks to our recipe testers: Garth Bixler, Mary Burkhart, Patricia Krueger, Elspeth Martin, Serena Moe, Sue Sutherland, and Ellen Ulf.

Many thanks especially to our beloved Nan Haynes and Cheryl Dobbins for keeping the home fires burning with a Cowgirl can-do attitude while we worked on this book.